PARTICIPATORY DEVELOPMENT :
Issues and Lessons

PARTICIPATORY DEVELOPMENT : *Issues and Lessons*

Dr. K. Muraleedharan

SERIALS PUBLICATIONS
NEW DELHI

First Published : 2006

ISBN : 81-86771-88-3

Published by

Head Office : SERIALS PUBLICATIONS
4, B.S.S. Hall, Khyber Pass Market
Civil Lines, Delhi-110054 (India)
Phone : 23245225
Fax : 91-11-23272135
E-mail: serials@satyam.net.in

Branch Office : 4830/24, Prahlad Street, Ansari Road
Darya Ganj, New Delhi-110002 (India)

To my mother,
Who left me alone in the midst of the
Works of this book

Acknowledgements

This work is a partial outcome of the couple of research projects the author has conducted in the broad area of Participatory Development and Empowerment of Women in the background of participatory development experiments in Kerala in 1996 through 2001. The support from individuals and institutions, that were instrumental in conceiving and conducting these research projects and bringing out the result in the form of a book length publication, is gratefully acknowledged.

The research projects were supported by (1) Ministry of Development Co-operation, Government of Netherlands and Kerala Research Programme on Local Level Development, Centre for Development Studies, Thiruvananthapuram, Kerala and (2) Sunya Foundation, Ahamedabad, Gujarat. The support and encouragement extended by these institutions are deeply acknowledged. The first project has been triggered off at the initiative and encouragement from Dr. K. Narayanan Nair, Director. CDS, Thiruvannthapuram, Kerala and the second one at the instance of Mr. Sivakumar, Sunya Foundation. Gujarat.

Dr. John Matthai Centre, University of Calicut, Aranattukara, Thrissur, Kerala has fostered and shaped the researcher in me. My Professors, Dr. P. P. Pillai and Dr. K. R. Lakshmy Devi, were instrumental in this process. Their constructive interventions have enriched the project as well as this work. I have taxed much from Dr. C. Krishnan and Dr. Vineetha Menon, who patiently sat with our research team at the discussion and orientation sessions. Mrs. Rajani Menon and Mrs. Nisha Varrier, Research Assistants of both these projects, had squeezed much out of themselves while wrestling with the field work and data collection. The critical comments from experts at Centre for Development Studies, Thiruvananthapuram, Kerala. NIRD, Hyderabad and ISEC, Nagarbhavi, Bangalore was of much use. The work has extracted much from the discussion with Dr. P. Ibrahim, Professor and Head, Dept of Economics, Pondicherry University, Mahe. Dr. Indira, Reader in Economics, Mysore University has patiently gone through the entire draft and offered comments.

The research projects and the current work have drawn much from the resources of 1) Population Council, John Hopkins University, 2) ELDIS Gender Reports, Institute of Development Studies, Sussex 3) WID Publication Series, Women and International Development Program, Michigan State University and 4) International Institute for Population Sciences, Mumbay. The assistance and support from Ms. Mandy Brown, Client Laison Officer, Popline Data Centre, John Hopkins University, Claudia Townsent, ELDIS Programme, Institute of Development Studies, Sussex and Tara L. Hefferan, Managing Editor, WID Publication Series, Women and International Development Program Michigan State University and Dr .C. P. Prakasam, Data Centre Incharge, IIPS, Mumbai are worth special mentioning.

The inferences and conclusions of this work have formed part of seminar papers presented at various venues like 1) Centre for Development Studies, Thiruvananthapuram, Kerala. 2.) National Institute of

Rural Development, Hyderabad, 3.) International Conference on Democratic Decentralisation, Thiruvananthapuram, Kerala, and various thematic seminars organized by Kerala Research Programme on Local Level Development. The suggestions and critical comments from the participants were quite enriching. Some of the inferences have appeared in the form of research papers in the journals like Calicut University Research Journal Asian Economic Review and a couple of edited volumes.

The Serial Publications, New Delhi deserves all the credit for bringing out this work in this present form. I am truly obliged to Mr. Jha for bringing out this work within the shortest period of time.

My mother, whom I lost amidst this work, used to recharge me with her delicious dishes while eating the boredom of 'sitting in front of my PC'. The contribution of my life partner Sarala, with her creative involvement and supportive nature, remains unfathomable. I really owe much to my kids who spared my papers and disks unharmed during their sneaks to my workplace. They lost my presence a lot while it was essential. I thank God for making me do all these. For all the errors crept in, I blame myself and no-one else.

Dr. K. Muraleedharan

Foreword

In recent years 'Participatory Development' has emerged as the most popular and accepted development strategy. It has replaced several conventional development paradigms in a big way. One can find an enormous corpus of literature on several theoretical and empirical aspects of it. Participatory Development is a unique strategy, and one can hardly do extremely well in it, since each experiment encounters fresh challenges and offers fresh lessons as well. It is often portrayed as a task that one has to learn by doing, and only doing. What Robert Chambers, the living legend on Participatory Development, observed in this context, is fitting. What the theory holds and what the reality offers are apparently poles apart. Hence each and every effort in this direction offers fresh lessons to those who are interested in the theory and practice of participatory development. The decentralized development experiment of Kerala since 1996 is extremely relevant in this context in terms of the issues it raises and the lessons it offers. The present volume prepared by a researcher, who is well exposed to the whole experiment, is a welcome addition to the literature on Kerala's experiment on participatory development. I have no hesitation to say that it is an innovative one in all aspects, though I do conflict with some qualifiers the author has extensively engaged to picturise the programme.

The development experiment of Kerala, as it unfolded, began to attract attention of scholars and development practitioners. Several scholars and development practitioners have been associating directly and indirectly with the experiment in diverse roles. Some of them have put their reflections in black and white from diverse perspectives. Hardly such an attempt can be traced that seeks to look at the episode from the perspective of participatory development. Thus, rather than the content, it is the perspective that makes this work unique and a worthy contribution towards development literature.

Participation, as has been mentioned, continues to reign and rule the development practice as well as debate. It is perpetually being enriched by experts and practitioners in a variety of ways. Perhaps the trickiest issue, often neglected, is the perspective of the participant and non-participant on it. Unless the practitioner is able to capture it, the design he prepares for mobilizing the mass is likely to be in the wrong direction and the programme is bound to be derailed. Therefore, an attempt of this type has to address such issues in length and this work does it fairly well.

Though the focus of the book is on the issues observed and lessons drawn from the participatory development experiment in Kerala, the author has shed light on the evolution of the development strategy of decentralization, participatory development, gendering development, empowerment of women and so on. The introductory chapters provide a clear understanding about the conceptual cob-webs and the background in which the campaign for people's planning was introduced. This has set the right frame work that further enables the reader to capture what follows. The detailed account of the Kerala model and the background for the launching of the campaign, the imperative of the campaign and the contextual interpretations were, though they seem to be a topic out of the scheme, have found the right place in the logical sequencing of the work.

The study has deeply gone into the issues of participatory development. The dynamics and determinants of participation, the quality of participation, motives behind true participation, and barriers to participation and promoting factors of participation were analyzed. The author has attempted to make some suggestions of policy relevance. It is hoped that this work will, therefore, be of much use for the policy makers and planners in the area of participatory development as well as for students of development economics.

Dr. P. P. Pillai

Director,

Institute of Planning and Applied Economic Research
Dr. John Matthai Foundation, University of Caliut
Aranttukara, Thrissur – 680618, Kerala, India

Contents

Acknowledgements v

Foreword ix

1. Introduction : *Towards a Participatory Regime* 1
2. Concepts, Definitions and Methodology 45
3. The Kerala Experiment : An Overview 70
4. Participatory Development in Kerala : An Assessment 113
5. Participatory Development : Issues and Lessons 165

Bibliography 177

1

Introduction :

Towards a Participatory Regime

This is the age of 'Participation' and it is the 'Paradigm of People' that rules and reigns the development debate. (Chambers 1994: Oakely 1991). Despite the theoretical setbacks and the practical problems, the canonical status attained by Participatory Approach to Development (PAD) sustains as an orthodoxy in development strategy and perhaps this might have invoked the seldom exaggerating remarks such as 'one can hardly find a development strategy without an element of participation' (Bastian 1997: Stirrat 1997). The evidences of this approach being put into practice from countries like South Korea, Singapore, Cuba, Sri Lanka, Costa Rica, China and India stand testimony to this. Apparently, there is a rush of literature on conceptual cob webs, critical assessment and experience sharing across the globe. (Brohman 1996: Burkey 1993: Chambers 1994: Escobar 1995: Mosse 1995: Vettivel 1999: Bastian 1997: Starkloff 1997: Stirrat 1997: Abdul Aziz : Andrea Cornwall: Andrea Wilkes: Fung and Wright: Hindson and Ngqulunga: Francois Pierre-Louis: Gianpaolo Baiocchi 2000: Isaac 1997,1999, 2000 : Isaac and Tharakan 1995: Isaac and Harilal 1997: John

Harris; John .T. Milimo 2000: Kurian 1999: Mungai Lenneiye 2000: Muraleedharan,K 2000a, 2000b, 2000c, 2001, 2002: Patrik Heller: Zesuliwe Mkhize 2000). As most of the experts argue, despite the aims of participatory development to involve people in development that affects them directly, surprisingly little attention is paid to understanding who wants to 'participate', what makes their participation possible, and what is in it for them. The basic question faced by those who are in the attempts to facilitate participation is that how the tempo of participation, if it has been triggered off successfully, can be sustained and how the strength of participation can be enhanced. Naturally, this question seeks the determinants of participation i.e., what actually drives one to development activities and what deters others from actively participating in development activities. Quite often, as Chambers puts it, the reality of participation sharply differs from the rhetoric, on many counts.(Chambers, 1999). This work, is an attempt to understand what theory holds and where the reality stands, as far as popular participation in development is concerned. In fact, this work has largely drawn from a couple of research projects in the area of participatory development and empowerment of women, conducted in the backdrop of Kerala's experiments with participatory development.

It may be interesting and useful to sketch the evolution of Participatory approach as well as Gendering of Development, as a development strategy, in its historical perspective for a better understanding of the current paradigm shift and its significance. Hence, this chapter serves to explore the evolution of development strategy over the last couple of decades and sketch the attempts for decentralisation, participation, integrating women in to development and empowerment at grassroots, leaving the conceptual cobwebs and experience sharing for a detailed discussion in the second chapter.

EVOLUTION OF ALTERNATIVE DEVELOPMENT STRATEGIES

The concept of human development is as old as Philosophy.[1] The question of what makes a good life had been haunting much of the ancient Philosophy. *Eudaimonie,* i.e. the state of having an objectively desirable life has been the deep concern of ancient Greek tradition including Aristotle. (Honderich 1995). Unfortunately, the ancient Greek Philosophy and subsequent moral theories have relatively less influence on the modern political economy and development economics that evolved during the 50's as well. The concept of *Eudaimonie* and the idea of human flourishing have made economists largely uncomfortable and they preferred to divorce their science from the realm of politics and moral philosophy. Human beings remained outside the scope of development and consequently little attention was devoted to the development of human being as an end in itself. Now a day, as a result of the attempts of economists like Sen, Huq, Hicks and Streeten, development efforts have been made to roam around people. The development has been redefined and redesigned with man at the centre.[2]

The experiences of 50s and 60s have apparently brought out the failures of the mainstream strategies and the need for an alternative development strategy. There has been wide dissatisfaction with the focus of development, measurement of it and even the concept of it. (Black 1991: Chenery et.al 1984: Huq 1976). Along with the arguments from the part of development experts, the intervention of international agencies led to the emergence of decentralization and participation as development strategies.[3] Parallel trends in radical development studies also stood in favor of this approach. Post-Marxian groups as well as Neo-Liberals have viewed empowerment as a strategy for fighting the disempower-ing activities of both the State and the markets through collective mobilisations of the marginalised groups (Loclan and Mouffee 1996: Mayo and Craig 1995: Paulo Fraire 1996: Stokke 1998). Mohan and Stokke (2000) have identified different versions of populist develop-ment thoughts, in between these two most prominent strands. For e.g. that of Chambers argue for reversing the previous centralism, in which all efforts will have to promote grassroots development. However, in all these cases, the basic focus is on localised, non capitalist practices. (Gibson - Graham 1995).

The central focus of mainstream strategies has been economic growth and top-down diffusion of development impulses. Growth was treated as the exclusive function of investment, and the benefits of development were expected to trickle down to the neediest sectors of society. Popular participation was confined to the ratification meetings in which outside experts used to brief the local people. By the end of 1960s, it was recognized that growth was not necessarily correlated with other development objectives such as rapid employment creation, reduction of poverty and inequality and provision of basic human needs. Severe maldevelopment problems were found to be appearing in some countries like Brazil, Iran, Kenya, Mexico, Nicaragua, Pakistan and South Africa. It was found that mere economic growth failed in eradicating poverty or providing jobs or reducing inequalities, as it was expected. There has been accumulating evidences for growing unemployment (Turnham 1971) increasing inequalities (Adelman and Morris 1973) and it has been argued that growth is followed by increased inequalities (Griffin 1989).

The development experiences of 50s and 60s have taught that mere growth was insufficient to induce broad based development and more than a decade of rapid development in underdeveloped countries has been of little or no benefit to perhaps a third of their population (Chenery et, al 1984). Economic growth had simply failed to filter down and the argument that top down development as well as trickle down strategies will alleviate widespread impoverishment has been questioned. A growing number of theorists and experts began to argue that the focus of macro economic growth had been misplaced, as the focus has been on the inanimate, instead of animate. (Black, 1991). Even the measurement of development has to be redefined in terms of people oriented criteria. It was the wide consensus on the fact that new development approaches should be oriented towards the satisfaction of basic human needs and desires particularly at the local community level that made Huq to observe that development should be built around people rather than make people roam around development (Mahbub.Ul Huq 1976).

As Stohr and Tailor (1981) put, it was expected that growth and development would proceed in a dispersed manner from below, by targeting at the poor and adopting programs suitable for local needs and requirements rather than following the conventional top down strategies. Rapid and more appropriate development forms can be evolved by encouraging participatory decision making and releasing the latent energies and creativity of the poor. Though a few isolated, but halted attempts to introduce the alternative development strategies can be traced even before 50s, the movement gathered momentum only after 70s when the international aid giving agencies began to intervene. (Bernstein and Campbell 1985: Moser 1987).

Dissatisfaction with the mainstream development models led to a frantic search for alternative people oriented approaches and consequently efforts were made to uncouple the direct exclusive relationship between growth and development, to consider the question of distributional equity, poverty, basic needs provision and adoption of appropriate technologies. A rather broad, eclectic, loosely defined new populist ideology gained much currency among the experts. (Kitching, 1982). The effect was to redefine the aim of development towards fostering fairer distribution of income and resources, encouraging local participation and promoting socially and environmentally appropriate technologies. A range of alternative development frame works has emerged during the recent years under the influence of both Neo-liberalism and other mainstream development strategies. Emphasise was shifted to projects which directly targeted at the poor, particularly the rural poor. Despite the theoretical rhetoric placed on community participation, a top-down social engineering approach continued to characterise development projects. Sincere and concrete attempts to empower popular organisations to take a more active role in political and economic decision-making were largely avoided. (Hettne 1990).

The major thrust of alternative development approach was basic needs. There have been different interpretations and varying concepts of basic needs, which were later transformed in to political claim for entitlements regarding the poor as people actively engaged in the struggle to define their own lives and means of livelihood. This approach no longer regards poor as passive victims of outside aid and has identified the role they play in alleviating poverty. Demanding greater popular participation, this approach, on the one hand, argued for a drastic change in the structure and organisation of institutions and agencies involved in development programmes, and on the other, the attainment of poor to become more organised and self-reliant. It is at these levels, the basic needs approach tend to become highly politicised, tied to issues of representation, participation and empowerment.

In the context of relationship between growth and inequality, that alternative strategy has a major deviation from the mainstream strategy. The mainstream development strategy has identified inequality and the resultant higher investment potential as the precondition for growth. However, the alternative development strategies that emerged in the seventies assumed that there need not be any conflict between growth and redistribution measures, and hence asserted for redistribution prior to growth. Redistribution measures proposed in alternative development strategies have three distinct approaches, as Griffin (1989) and Emmerie (1987) observed. First, there were strategies that stressed on employment intensive measures for the working poor. Second, there were measures that linked growth with redistribution by advocating measures that would transfer an increasing part of increments to total income that would arise from accelerated growth to the poor. Thirdly, there were strategies that focused on the elaboration of basic needs approach, placing greater emphasise on helping the poor to acquire more economic and political power.

The Cocoyock Declaration of (1974) has triggered off the drive for alternative frameworks of development while the urge for it has been sustained by two other international efforts. viz,. First, the documents published by Swedish Dag Hammerskjold Foundation in 1975, which had outlined a more humanistic approach to development and second, the International

Foundation for Development Alternatives (IFDA) by promoting an alternative bottom-up approach to development coined as the 'Third System project of 1976'. The Third System project was an attempt to explore new methods of raising consciousness and increasing participation by grassroots movements in development decision making. The approach has clearly made distinction between the First System- the State, the Second System- the transnational capital and the Third System -People's Power, which constituted people acting individually and collectively through voluntary institutions as well as social movements.

At least in theory and to a certain extent in practice, there has been some emphasise on local participation. Emphasise was particularly given to fostering local institutions to enhance people's participation in the selection, design and management of development projects at the community level. Participation was viewed as an important end in itself, also it was linked to a number of other instrumental values as Griffin (1989) puts it. First, participation in community-based organisations could help to identify local priorities so that development projects might better reflect grass root needs and wishes. Participation in popular organisations and groups, co-operatives, land reform committees, irrigation societies, women organisations might assist in mobilising local support for development projects and programmes. Thirdly, increased local participation might reduce the cost of many public services and development projects by shifting more responsibility to grassroots organisations.

Mohan and Stokke (2000) have clearly sketched the evolution of development strategy during the last couple of decades, critically examining the links between development theory and political action and the ways in which new political spaces are being created. Development, as they argue, has been a movement from holistic theorisation towards more empirically informed and inductive approaches. Simultaneously, movement towards participation and empowerment has led to the emergence of the 'local' as the site of empowerment, knowledge generation and development intervention. The two major intellectual streams that have contributed towards this development thinking and intervention, according to them, are the Neo liberalism and Post-Marxism.

Development Economics has traditionally assigned a key role to the interventionist state in correcting market failures and ensuring economic efficiency, growth, stability as well as social development. A dramatic shift in this paradigm was brought by the neo-liberal counter-revolution in development theory and the state came to be viewed as a barrier than a driving force in the development process. (Toye. J 1987). The 80 has witnessed strong critical observations about the role of the State and promoted market liberalism as the most efficient mechanisms for delivering economic and social development. Recently the singular emphasise on markets has been shifted to additional emphasise on institutional reforms. (WB, 1997). Civil Society has emerged as the arena in which development objectives are to be achieved. According to Hyden (1997), civil societies, as the neo-liberalists perception goes, can exert organised pressure on autocratic state and unresponsive governments to ensure democratic stability and good governance. Civil society institutions have been identified as the vehicles for participation of people and empowerment of them. This has offered tuff challenges to the top-down diffusion of State planning.

Parallel trends can be viewed in more radical development studies. Post-Marxian groups have viewed empowerment as a strategy for fighting the disempowering activities of both the State and the markets through collective mobilisations of the marginalised groups. Still there are critical differences between the conceptuali-sation of development between Neo - liberals and Post-Marxians.(Stokke, 1998). The Neo-liberals conceptualise participation and empowerment as a harmony model of power in which efforts are taken by the State agencies to collaborate the Non-governmental institutions to make the efforts of State more efficient and to include identified target groups in the process of development. This implies that the empowerment of powerless can be achieved within the existing social order hardly affecting the power of the powerful negatively.(Mayo and Craig 1995).

In contrast to this view of revisionist neo-liberalists, the Post Marxian radical notion of empowerment focus on bottom up social mobilisation in a society as a challenge to hegemonic interests within the State and Market. The key elements in this process are conscientisation and collective identity formation around common experience within economic and political marginalisation. (Paulo Fraire 1996). Power is conceptualised as both in relational and conflictual terms. According to Laclan and Mouffee (1996) empowerment of the marginalised requires transformation of economic and political relationship towards radically democratized society. Mayo and Craig (1995) opine that both these strands of development thoughts share the common perception that State and Markets cannot and should not be solely held responsible for ensuring equality and social justice with fair rates of growth. Second, local knowledge, actors and interventions are the key factors in both these strands of thought. Mohan and Stokke(2000) also identify different versions of populist development thoughts, in between these two most prominent strands. For e.g. that of Chambers argue for reversing the previous centralism and all development efforts have to promote grassroots development. However, in all these cases, the basic focus is on localised, non-capitalist practices. (Gibson - Graham 1995).

ATTEMPTS FOR DECENTRALISATION

Another major thread of the development framework during the post-war period was the thrust for decentralisation. Along with the acceptance of alternative development strategies, there has been a tendency in the third world countries to decentralise their planning as the aftermath of wide dissatisfaction with the Keynesian development planning during the 60s and 70s. As Browman(1996) observes, though the concept of decentralised planning suffered a set back during the eighties, the ideas of decentralisation and local level participation were in favor during the 90s, both in theory and practice.

The emergence of new wave of enthusiasm in democratic decentralisation can be traced to the late 80's, when many of the developing countries, either on their own or under the influence of international donors agencies, started experimenting with the idea of democratisation of local governance. During the early 1990s, large number of programmes for strengthening democratic local governance was launched in various countries.

Louis (2000) has observed that, decentralisation, as a concept to hold government more accountable to population, has gained popularity in developing countries, primarily in those that are experiencing democratic transition. Many governments perceived it as a means through which power can be shared among factions and through which resources can be allocated efficiently to various groups in society. Cohen and Peterson (1999) identified the root of this tendency to go for decentralised governance on the initiative of international aid agencies to insist on progressively introducing decentralisation, devolution of powers to local bodies and popular participation, in the aid receiving countries. Campbell (1997) describes decentralisation as quite a revolution in Latin America. He observes that, the changes in government associated with decentralisation are thought to hold the potential to deepen democracy, make for more accountable and efficient institution, increase citizens input and foster co-operation, across the public and private divide.

It is a fact that there has been different definitions given to the decentralisation with multiple meanings such as deconcentration, devolution, delegation etc. each having different programmes and objectives. (Samof, 1990) Some of the analysts have taken it as administrative decentralisation and some others have taken it radically as political decentralization - a means to empower previously underrepresented or marginal groups. The administrative decentralisation while concentrates on wider distribution of infrastructure and services, political decentralisation aims at actual transfer of decision-making authority to local representatives of the popular majority and focus on empowerment and participation of people at large. This is what we encounter in certain experiments in the Third World countries.[4]

Slater (1989) has observed that the term decentralisation can be articulated in to a monetarist discourse, but alternatively it can be linked to a discussion that combines ideas of collective empowerment, and participation in a managerial state. He adds that decentralisation holds up the promise of a reordering of political space and revitalisation of "local" in terms of democracy and socialism. Mohan (1996) argues that decentralisation has become an underlying principle in this move towards more technocratic accountability and choice. In fact, it constitutes a fluid, a flexible discourse that can be utilised by different ideological interests. Particularly, World Bank (1990) have promoted decentralisation as a means of breaking the power of central ministries, increasing revenue generation, shifting the burden of service delivery on to local stake holders. However, this approach to decentralisation promoted by World Bank, is entirely different compared to liberal as well as radical approaches that see devolution of power to local governments as a means of promoting a new communitarian spirit and forming the seedbed of democratic process. According to Mohan (2000) the underpinnings of this vision of decentralisation is "Rational Choice Theory" (RCT) which permits a more political readings of decentralisation to be transferred to a narrative of capital and efficiency.

Cheema and Rondinelli (1983) view decentralisation as the transfer of planning decision or administrative authority from the central governments to its field organisations, local administrative units, semi-autonomous and local governments and NGOs. Kochen and Deutsch (1980) were more concerned with efficiency in policy formulation and more specifically in the output of organisational service system. According to them, the core of decentralisation in a service system is its responsiveness, the shortness of its communication time and the directness of its channels between servers and clients.

Randinelli et .al (1989) attempts to develop a "new" political economy framework for analyzing decentralisation programmes. In his framework, either the State is viewed in terms of "constraining" or "enabling" and society is reduced to the characteristics of people as consumers. The organisational arrangements for decentralisation include privatisation, deregulation, delegation and devolution of powers. It is criticised that this model ignores the other dimension of decentralisation namely, the notion of participation and empowerment.

Chandrasekher (2000) has observed that planning would appear a contradiction in terms of the adherent of classical role and nature of planning in economic system. At the core of the orthodox literature on planning, one can find a process of centralised investment decision making, which had its corollary central access to and allocation of the surplus available in the system. Decentralisation, as he views, if it is to be meaningful, it requires the devolution of resources as well as power.

Baiocchi (2000) argues that decentralisation can have many different meanings, but in the context of policy advocacy, it means at its broadest, as it involves, the shifting of government functions and responsibilities away from central agencies to local ones. The author adds that, the net result of decentralisation in developing world is not clear, though the literature is replete with success stories involving specific instances of local reform that not only improve the delivery of services and revitalising local civic involvement. Decentralisation will, by itself, hardly ensure these benefits, but it is clear that decentralisation of government has been accompanied by a hollowing out of State. Baiocchi also adds that in most of the South, decentralisation has been introduced in most inauspicious circumstances, as a mandate to comply with measures of IMF. Fiscal austerity measures have been the single exclusive determinant as well as motivator for decentralisation attempts.

According to Turner and Hulme (1997) decentralisation through devolution is the approach in which the citizen participation has emerged. This form of decentralisation is hailed as the ideal form of decentralisation as it combines the promise of local democracy and technical efficiency. Examining the efforts of Political decentralisation in Africa, Tordoff (1994) argues that, Political decentralisation in Africa denote the devolution of powers or representative local councils, each with its separate legal existence and its own budget and with the authority to allocate resources to carry multiple functions. Decentralisation thorough devolution, in essence, transfer powers from the central authority to the local level through institutional structures that can guarantee effective citizen participation.

Litrack and Jessica (1999) have noted that in a decentralised devolved system all local bodies have clear and legally recognised geographical boundaries over which they exercise and within they perform public functions. Jha (1997) has opined that there have been consistent suggestions for division and dispersal of power, which the ubiquitous phenomena of concentration of power in institution as well as individuals was explained. Democracy and democratisation have given renewed emphasise on decentralisation.[5]

Smith (1985) has argued that advocacy for decentralisation has been a part of liberal political tradition. It is clear that decentralisation is beneficial for the functioning of democratic system at the national as well as local level.

As far as the forces that compelled the introduction of decentralisation are concerned, Crook and Mannuel (1998) have observed that along with the size and complexity of the territory, religion, language, economic development and cultural enclave have played their role. In other words, pressures both from above and below thus effect decentralisation.

It is interesting to examine why decentralisation was argued. There are a vide variety of arguments for Decentralisation. The reduced cost of information (Marshach and Marschak 1959), optimum units and better results (Chakravarthy 1972: Mathur 1973) the advantages of sub-system planning (Dutta Choudhury 1973) homogeneity in planning units (Boudeville 1996) and appropriate strategy for planning in a country with wide regional variations in all aspects like India (Gadgil 1967: Raj 1971: Biswas 1973: Mathur 1973: Aziz 1983: Jain et.al 1985: Ghosh 1988: Gulati 1994). Raj (1971) has stressed on the better opportunities of local people's participation in planning and Aziz (1993) and Webster (1994) have focused on overcoming the 'departmentalism' in the plan formulation in India.

Decentralisation helps to diminish regional inequalities, reduce inefficiency and waste, promote more appropriate development of human as well as natural resources, alleviate poverty by redistributive measures and facilitate more effective implementation of plans and improve local responsiveness and participation. Conyers (1985) has opined, decentralisation has been viewed as a means to transform political and administrative systems to make them more efficient, more appropriate to local conditions and more responsive to changing needs of socio-economic and spatial development. Agreeing with this, Maro (1990) asserts that decentralisation is regarded as a vital

technique to facilitate local participation in development projects, increase flexibility and efficiency, create consensual support for development initiatives needed to promote national unity and political stability.

Isaac and Franke (2000) have examined in what ways democratic decentralisation can contribute towards economic growth and welfare of the people. According to them, the traditional economic theory has focused on the advantages of local decision making due to several reasons as highlighted by Oates (1972), Musgrave (1959) and Marschak (1959). Since economic development is regarded as the duty of the local bodies, local level planning becomes essential not only to respond to the preferences of the local people, but also for the efficient utilisation of resources of all kinds. This will do away with the evils of concentration like duplication, lack of complementarity and narrow departmentalism.

Democratic decentralisation also ensures efficiency in implementation as well as transparency and participation. It provides a check on misuse of resources and better monitoring, as there is participation by people directly in the implementation process. The dormant resources so far left unused will be mobilised and put to their most efficient use through democratic decentralisation. Isaac and Franke link the democratic decentralisation experiments in Kerala with the concept of Social Capital. Quoting Ellikson(1991) and Evans (1997) the authors conclude that democratic decentralization has the potential for nurturing useful state-civil society synergies.(Isaac and Franke, 2000).

There is a wide apprehension among a few neo-liberal theorists that decentralisation will definitely downsize the State. Baiocchi (2000) feels that it will hollow the State. However, Fung and Wright (2000) have, as quoted by Isaac and Franke (2000), observed that democratic decentralisation, in fact, makes the State more effective and "decentralisation of the State apparatus is essential for transforming the existing state institutions into empowered deliberative bodies." As far as the authors are concerned, decentralisation is viewed as the instrument to widen and deepen democracy.

Patnaik (2000) has observed that decentralisation and strengthening of local administration bodies through devolution of decision making and resources, is not a part of rolling back of the state, but a means of enforcing greater accountability on the part of the state, by entrusting a whole range of decision which directly effect the lives of people, to these layers of the State where the people can organise effective supervision over it. Arun Ghosh (2000) feels that decentralisation in decision-making has become a political or economic pattern of governance and there is no retreat from steps taken in this regard. He is optimistic that decentralisation efforts enacted any where will harbinger a new pattern of economic thinking. Slater(1989) has observed that decentralisation can be articulated in to a monetarist discourse, but alternatively it can be linked in to a discourse of ideas of collective empowerment, democracy and socialism.

However, as the studies on recent development initiatives suggest that attempts on decentralisation have failed to bring out the desired results. In many cases, the rhetoric has been much ahead of actual practice. (Khan 1987: Vengroff and Johnson 1989: Baiocchi, 2000). Inspite of the trumpeting on democractic decentralisation, people's power and local autonomy, very few genuine attempts have been made to implement them. (Simon and Rakodi, 1990) Political committment towards decentralisation has been marginal. In the case where political decentralisation has occurred, the power has been concentrated with the local elites. More over, most of the decentralised planning has been given inadequate human and material resources to fulfill their functions (Browman, 1996).

The attempts of decentralisation in India can be traced back to the early 40s, by the pioneer of Indian planning, Sir Visheshwaraya. (Isaac and Franke, 2000). The planning commission took the first step to decentralisation in 1969 in the form of guidelines for the Formulation of District Plans. The attempts for decentralisation in Kerala dates back to late 50s when the administrative reforms committee recommended various measures towards devolution of powers.(Isaac and Tharakan, 1995). Unfortunately, the recommendations were not implemented as the government was dismissed. A significant step in this direction was taken in 1987-91, when the district councils were created. The recent experiments of People's Campaign for Planning are undoubtedly a great leap towards decentralisation and empowerment of people at grass root level. The World Bank Mission recently visited India has assessed this programme, as a unique experiment, in which three million or roughly 10 per cent of the population of the State has participated directly in the planning process. (George Mathew 1999).

PARTICIPATION IN DEVELOPMENT

As we have seen, the efforts to sketch out an alternative development strategy have culminated in the efforts for decentralisation as well as participation.[6] In other words, the decade long search for development strategy has hooked the development debate into two orthodoxies viz. Structural Adjustment Policy and Participatory Development. While the former addresses the question of economic growth, the latter addresses the issues of poverty and distribution in the context of capitalist development. The current scenario of development debate is being dominated by these two orthodoxies. Perhaps, this might have evoked critical remarks that one can hardly find a development model without an element of Participation. Stirrat (1997) was not extravagant when he observed that such is the popularity of the concept that it is now difficult to find a rural based development project which does not claim to adopt a participatory approach involving bottom-up planning, acknowledging the importance of indigenous knowledge and local people.

It is quite an undisputed fact that Participation, basically which connotes taking part or sharing has wide implications in the development context as it goes further to the question of who shares, with whom and in which context. Samaranayake (1997) has observed that Participation has a long history as various governmental as well as non-governmental organizations, both at the national and international level have been focusing on since the last two decades.

There are different schools of thought that hold strikingly different, and some of them often conflicting, views about the emergence and evolution of Participatory Approach to Development. One of the prominent arguments, most often quoted and popularised by staunch critics of Participatory Approach like Stirrat, runs like this. (Stirrat 1997) Along with the discourse in Economics, the disillusionment with the radical leftist policies also contributed towards the emergence and popularisation of Participation in Development as an alternative strategy. Generally, two factors were held responsible for this. First, failure of leftist political parties in bringing about the required transformation of society and second, the limitations of the State-centered policies pursued so far by the traditional political parties. All these resulted in a wild search for a better mode of intervening in politics. Consequently, People's movement was put foreword as an entirely different strategy in Politics.

The evolution of this strategy according to Mallika Smarnayake (1997) has been an outcome of the existed gap between the planners and beneficiaries. The development intervention of 70s identified two types of actors. On the one side, were those who engaged in the task of identifying development needs, planning development activities, mobilising resources for development and implementing programmes. On the other hand were the beneficiaries of development who marginally involved in the development drama. They represented who do the things and for whom the things are being done. This particular relationship between these two groups has been characterised by mistrust and antagonism that led to a gap between them that remained unbridged so far. The process of development activities undertaken makes the marginal involvement of the beneficiaries clear and talks about the grave negligence of the genuine needs of the people for whom the programmes were conceived and implemented. The availability of funds and other considerations ruled the whole process. Consequently, the rural development projects were thrown incomplete at midway due to the hostile attitude of the beneficiaries (Cohen and Uphoff 1971). Participatory methodologies evolved to bridge the gap between the two sectors, beneficiaries and planners.

John Kurian (1997) puts the evolution and emergence of Participatory approach differently. According to him, Participatory development, its emergence and evolution has been a movement of development debate from its focus on goods and services to highlight the prime role that public participation plays in the process. Participation has been added as a fresh ingredient of development. Phrases such as planning from below, involving the people, incorporating people's knowledge are part of the emerging common orthodoxy of development. A sharp sense of distrust and skepticism about all the top-down process of development particularly that by the State has been the common thread with this new approach to development. It also hardly spares the bureaucracy, which is being viewed with strong suspicion, and western knowledge and technology. Strictly, it is a strategy working through Non-government organisations or micro level interventions to empower people, which is expected to effect a macro change in the economy. Sen (1989) in this context has rightly observed that public action and popular participation has pressured the State and the interest that dominated it to provide facilities that contributed to a reasonable level of well being for the people and the opportunities for advancement.

Starkoff (1997) agrees with the contention that Participation in development is an offshoot of radical politics. Both in affluent economies as well as in third world economies, democratisation of development activities has been one of the long-standing demands raised by the radicals. The major objective of this was to prevent the adverse impact of normal, bureaucratic and elite dominated development efforts on the disempowered and to generate receptiveness to the interests of the 'people'. The grass root movements precipitated by the waves of social movements in the second half of twentieth century throughout North America and Europe placed 'Participation in policy making and planning' as their first and foremost agenda. These grassroots actions were able to drew instantaneous and unstinted support from the intelligentsia of that times in the form of innovative ideas, tools and concepts like 'Pedagogy of the oppressed'[7], Participatory Action Research,[8] Local Knowledge etc. There has been strong criticism about the development process that failed to hit the targets or exploited its supposed beneficiaries by imposing projects from above. The strategies of research and development sought to involve the local people in the process of knowledge production and to combine research and community mobilization as the tools of social change. 'This has turned Participation to be a tool of social engineering, corollary to the engineering of the material world'.

Participatory and process driven social interventions have history that dates back to before 1945 as observed by Cook (1998). Vettivel (1999) argues that Participation is not a new concept, as far as rural development in India is concerned, and it has been talked and written about during 50s or even before. The earlier forms of participation in development were Shramdhan, (Voluntary Labour), Bhoodan (Donation of Land) and Gramadhan (Donation of Village). He clearly makes out the difference between Participation in Development and Participatory Development. The former according to him is a method to get the projects implemented by the people as 'they' participate in 'our' projects. Participatory development takes place when people are mobilized, organized over a long period to identify their local development problems, estimate the resources at their disposal, anlayse various options, set their goals and implement their projects. However, it is possible that both Participation in Development and Participatory Approach can be made a continuum. In other words, a project in which participation is envisaged can be made participatory later.

Early in the 50s, participation of people in development was confined to public cooperation in the form of cash contribution, land donations and voluntary labour contributions in the top - down development projects assigned to those who are willing. Panchayaths and Co-operatives were the important grassroots level organizations. The inherent structural impediments of these institutions and the social circumstances then existed posed heavy blocks in the ways of fostering participation. The caste-class hierarchical power relations, which remained unchallenged and unques-tionable, were the most important hindrances stood in the way of mass participation. Consequently, participa-tion was confined to election and voting alone. The entry of State as the monopolized custodian of resources put an end to the participation by contribution and then began the era of development planning in which State played a pivotal role as designer, mobiliser and controller of development programmes. The decadal long state initiative for development has left dilapidated public buildings, broken hand pumps, washed-out bridges, silted ponds and channels of water supply, pot holed roads etc. In this context, the remarks of Upholf and Cohen (1977) that an evaluation of the over 50 development projects that reveals that participation of beneficiaries is a crucial element in the successful implementation of them, are noteworthy. Samaranayake adds that due to lack of participation, a large number of development projects have resulted in short lived progress.

The mode of delivery of development fruits warranted the active involvement of the community and the efforts in this direction have to be geared in such a way that it makes people aware, recognizing the local wisdom in planning process and forming their organizations to implement the programme. Thus, participation in development gradually was transformed in to participatory development in which people and their resources were used for implementing projects. The steps included creating awareness and required capacity to maintain the public utilities created and essentially, it was an exercise to make the local people fit to the projects.

The entry of the social activist NGOs in the 70s to the field of development added a fresh dimension to the concept of participatory approach. The Socialist and Marxist ideologies, Paulo Frair's concept of Non-directional Education, Social Mobilisation – Pedagogy of the oppressed – were the catalytic elements, which framed the concept of Participatory development. Such groups like Kerala Sasthra Sahithya Parishad in Kerala, were the first people to talk about people's power and they had a strong mass base and were with non-political background. It is these groups first sow the seeds of participatory approach.

The emergence and evolution of Participatory approach is really a confluence of ideas and efforts at intellectual as well as practical level by expert in different disciplines. This has given it a multidisciplinary plane. Along with the emergence of Participatory Approach to Development, there has been a call for integrating women in to development in various ways. Women, who have been placed at the margins of development, considering them either as obstacles to development or passive beneficiaries of it, were seen slowly moving towards the mainstream during the recent decades. The discussion about the evolution of alternative development strategies, which culminated in participation of people, will be incomplete without a discussion on the enhanced role women have been ascribed in the theory and practice of development.

WOMEN IN DEVELOPMENT

Before 70s, Development theory as well as practice has been gender neutral, the role of women in development was invisible, and women and gender relations have been virtually ignored with in these frames. (Brohman 1996: Nussbaum 2003) In other words, they hardly distinguished between men and women assuming that development policies and programmes benefit all automatically, While, special programmes were designed to benefit women as mother and child bearer as well as targets of worst ravages of poverty and malnutrition. Unfortunately, women's role in agriculture and other productive sectors was left unperceived in the framework. As Parpart (1993) observes women were systematically excluded from various aspects of development, to the extent that they were regarded as impediments to development. Development theory and practice during the post-war period ignored women presuming that productive work was performed by men alone. Till recently, as Ahmed (1987) puts, rural development strategies have neglected the role of women. Elson(1991) observes that a strong male bias has been operating in development theories and programmes.

Seventies witnessed growing interest in making the framework of development theory gender sensitive. As Marilee Karl (1995) observed, it all began with the pioneering efforts of Ester Bosurup (Women's Role in Economic Development, 1970) with the efforts for making women active participants in production, household activities and other sectors of the society. It was understood that women have been often victims of development programmes, rather than beneficiaries. Most of the development programmes that were assumed to benefit everybody really benefited men only and often had negative effects on the women as well as on the whole community. The high rate of failures of these programmes were attributed to the neglect or lack of knowledge of women's productive as well as reproductive work.

Much of the impetus for rising interest in the role of women in development came from the U.N Decade for Women (1975-85) and the events accompanied it. It has considerably promoted and legitimised the women's movements at national level as well as international level (Hahner, 1985). As Geisler (1993) has observed, it has forced a rethinking of development policies which began to conceptualise women as agents of productive process and identified women's' marginalisation as the chief cause of their deteriorating status. The three women conferences organised during the last decades have delineated four major goals. Of them, three are related to various aspects of women and development. The documents came out of these conferences laid stress on linkages between Socio-Economic and Political conditions and called for the need of full participation and employment. The rise of 'Women in Development' approach has been the outcome of the conference, which linked, unlike the previous approaches, advancement of women with improved access to employment and educational structures. It argued that in order to overcome their historical marginalisation, women must be integrated with the development process.

The women in development policy (WID) which gained a footing during the later half of 70s has three distinct approaches according to Moser (1993). i.e., the equity approach, the anti-poverty approach and the efficiency approach. Maxine Molyneaux (1985) has examined how this approach has attempted to meet women's needs by distinguishing practical gender needs and strategic gender needs. The practical gender needs refers to what actually women needs to fulfill their role as tasks like training and childcare obligations. However, strategic gender needs are those that women require in order to overcome their subordination.

The equity approach, which Moser calls the original approach is deeply concerned with the unequal relations between men and women in the society. It places emphasise on the economic independence as synonymous with equity. In other words, the equity approach attempts to meet the women's practical gender needs for income and strategic gender needs for equality with men through top-down legislative interventions by government and development agencies. However, unfortunately, when implemented, the equity approach left out the strategic gender needs and concentrated on practical gender needs on the ground that equity programmes necessitated unacceptable interference with country's tradition. The anti-poverty approach, links the economic inequality of women with poverty and does not take into account the aspects of female subordination. The efficiency approach, which emerged in the 80s assumes that development can be made more efficient and effective by participating women, which is treated as equity.

Eighties witnessed a serious focus on women's unintended marginalisation in development programmes and forced to have a rethinking on WID approaches. There have been arguments for mainstreaming women to the center of development efforts from the margins of it. In addition, there have been concerns about the consequences of mainstreaming women such as it will loose the special focus and attention and will be thrown in to a male dominated world. Still there have been arguments for increasing women's participation in development process and ensuring that woman's perspectives and needs constitute the basis of the redefinition of development itself. Because of shift from 'integration of women in to development' to 'mainstreaming women' by mid 80's has been accompanied by a shift in focus from 'women' to 'gender'. The new approach, Gender and Development (GAD) approach identifies the role of women and men contextual to time, place and culture. The role of women and men are, to a certain extend, depending on the time, place and cultural aspects. Thus, the focus on gender has examined the roles and needs of men and women and how they are interrelated, there by reducing the risk of marginalising women. The GAD approach is said to have the potential to bring in women's vision of development as observed by the Canadian Council for International Cooperation. The Council states that Gender and Development is emerging as a progressive approach to development from Women's perspective and experiences. It is a part of the larger work of creating an alternative development model, for a Worldview that moves beyond an econo-mist's analysis to include environmental, sustainable and qualitative aspects in its definition of development. It needs to be noted that the GAD approach, unlike the WID approach, essentially differs in the sense that it does not question the prevailing development paradigm, examines the potential of interpreting it, and applying it according to the perceptions of women, observes Marrilee Karl (1995).

The empowerment approach gained popularity during the later half of 90s. Apart from the concept of empowerment as the emphasise of individualistic values like capacity and entrepreneurial skill, there has been interpretations of it in terms of participation in the policymaking and planning process. Generally two approaches commonly used by development agencies needs to be outlined in the context of empowerment. First, it is interpreted as empowerment through economic interventions to increase employment, income generation and access to credit and: Second empowerment through integrated rural development programmes, in which a comprehensive plan for the overall development of women is envisioned, of which income generation is a single component. This view of empowerment usually discards any role for women in defining her life and future. The popular version of empowerment, often shared one by the NGOs and action groups seems to be more radical and highly political in spirit as it envisions awareness building, capacity creation, organising women that leads to transformation of unequal relationships, increased decision making power in the home and community, and greater participation in politics.(Battliwala,1993). Some of these ideas have reflected in the policy and programmes of development agencies across the world. The evolution in policy on women and development has influenced what is happening at the grass root level. Many of the development agencies are gearing their programmes and projects towards empowerment of women through capacity building and ensuring women's participation at grass root level. Women's participation in grass root organisations is increasingly recognised as crucial to their empowerment and as a way for them to help shape development policies.

NOTES

1. For a detailed discussion on Ethics of the Concept of Development, see. David Alexander *Clark, Development Ethics: A Research Agenda,* Working Paper Series No. 110, Department of Economics, School of Oriental and African Studies, University of London, May 2000.
2. Sen.'s contribution towards the emergence of an alternative approach to development is catalytic. By the 90s, the capabiilty approach had emerged as the leading alternative to traditional concept of welfare. Sen's conceptual framework and friendship with the late Mahbub Ul Huq encouraged the UNDP to compile an annual series of Human Development Report, of which the first was drafted by Sen himself.

3. In addition to the World Bank and ILO, a number of organisations figured prominently in the creation of an alternative development agenda in 1970s, including the UNEP, UNCTAD,UNDP,UNRISD,UNICEF,WHO and FAO. Among the attempts of these organisations dedicated to design a fresh development agenda, the landmark was the conference held at Cocoyoc, Mexico in 1974. Bringing together the experts from various parts of the world, the conference looked in to the '*Patterns of resource use, Environment and Development Strategies*' and issued a manifesto called *'Cocoyok Declaration'* which stated that development efforts of the last decades have proved impossible to meet the inner limits of satisfying fundamental human needs while the number of human beings who are hungry and homeless were on the increase. Development efforts should address the fresh challenges like degradation of environment as well as the traditional one's like human needs and other considerations such as freedom of expression and self realisation. Hence, Hettne (1990: 152) has rightly remarked that the Cocoyoc Declaration has marked the birth of an "alternative" trend in development theory.
4. Fung and Wright have the right terminological choice for this real world decentralisation experiments as "Deliberative Empowered Democracies" and they sight five of them as the illustrative ones. They are 1.) Functionally Specific Neighbourhood Councils of Chicago, U.S.A 2).Wiscosin Regional Training Partnership 3.) Stake holders Eco System Governance under the U.S Endangered Species Act 1973. 4.) Participatory City Budgeting in Porto Alegre, Brazil and 5.) The Village Governance in West Bengal and Kerala's People's Campaign for Local Level Planning. For a detailed discussion of decentralisation in the context of democratisation see: Wright 2000 : Fishkin 1995 : Fung and Wright 2000.
5. For a detailed discussion of decentralisation in the context of democratisation see: Wright 2000 : Fishkin 1995 : Fung and Wright 2000.
6. For a detailed analysis and critical assessment of Participatory Development and Empowerment in the global/local world, see Parpart, 2000.

7. See Paulo Freir (1996) Pedagogy of the Oppressed, Penguin, Landon.
8. Literature on Research Methodology is replete with works on Participatory Action Research ever since it has been conceived.

REFERENCES

Adelman and Morris, (1973), *Economic Growth and Social Equity in Developing Countries.* Stanford: Stanford University Press.

Ahmed, I.,(1987), "Technology, Production Linkages and Women's Employment in South Asia" *International Labour Review*, 126, pp. 21-40.

Andrea Cornwall, Hentry Lucas and Kath Pasteur,(2000), "Accountability Through Participation: Developing Workable Partnership models in Health Sector". *IDS Bulletin*, Vol. 31, Number 1, January 2000, Institute of Development Studies, Sussex, pp. 1-14.

Andrea Wilkes, (2000), *"The Function of Participation in a Village Based Health Repayment Scheme : What can Participation Actually do ?" IDS Bulletin*, Vol. 31, Number 1, January 2000, Institute of Development Studies, Sussex, pp. 31-36.

Archon Fung and Errik Olin Wright, (2000), *"Deepening Democracy: Innovations in Empowered Participatory Governance".* Paper Presented at the International Conference on Democratic Decentralisation, May 2000, State Planning Board, Kerala.

Aziz , Abdul, (2000), "Democratic Decentralisation in Karnataka 'Paper Presented at the International Conference on Demo-cratic Decentralisation, May 2000, State Planning Board, Kerala.

——(1983), *Studies in Block Planning.* Concept, New Delhi.

Arun Ghosh, (2000), "Globalisation, Decentralisation and Economic Development" Paper Presented at the International Conference on Democratic Decentralisation, May 2000, State Planning Board, Thiruvananthapuram, Kerala.

Baiocchi, Gianpolo, (2000), "Synergising Civil Society. The Politics of Decentralisation in Poto Alegre, Brazil." Paper

Presented at the International Conference on Democratic Decentralisation, May 2000, State Planning Board, Kerala.

Bastian, Sunil and Bastian, Nicola, (Ed.) (1997), *Assessing Participation: A debate from South Asia*, New Delhi.

Battivala, S. "Empowerment of Women in South Asia : Concept and Practices" ASSBAF and FAO, Fredom from Hunger Campaign, Action and Development, 1993.

Bernstein, H. Campbell, B., (eds), (1985), *Contradictions of Accumulation in Africa*. Bverly Hills, C A: Sage.

Bandyopadhyay, D., (1997), People's Participation in Planning. Kerala Experiment.'*Economic and Political Weekly* Sep.27, pp. 2450-2454.

Bhattacharya, Dwaipayan, (2001), 'Human Development and Civic Community in India: Making Democracy Perform' *Economic and Political Weekly*, Vol.XXXVI, Feb 24, 2001, pp. 673-684.

Bergsten, Fred, C., (1993), "*The Rationale For a Rosy view*". The Economist Sept. 11, 1993.

Bhatnagar, B. and Williams, (1992), (ed.) "*Participatory Develop-ment and the World Bank, Potential Directions for Change*", World Bank Discussion Papers No.183, October 1992.

Biswas, Ajith, (1973), "Central Planning and its Regional Implications with Reference to West Bengal" Seminar Paper of Center for Social Science, 24 February 1974, Culcutta, Mimeo.

Black, (1991), *Development in Theory and Practice: Bridging the Gap* Boulder: Westview.

Boudeville, J.R., (1961), *Regional Economic Planning; Techniques of Analysis*, OECD, Paris.

Brohman, John, (1996), Popular Development: Rethinking the Theory and Practice of Development, Blackwell, Cambridge.

Burkey, S., (1993), *People First, A Guide to Self Reliant Participatory Rural Development*, London : Zed Books,Landon.

Campbell, T., (1997), Innovation and Risk Taking-The Engine of Reform in Latin American Countries, World Bank.

Chakravarthy, S., (1990), Development Strategies for Growth with equity: The South Asian Experience, Asian Development Review, 8, pp. 133-159.

Chambers, R., (1994), "*Paradigm Shifts and the Practice of Participatory Development*", *IDS Working Papers No. 2, Institute of Development Studies, Sussex.*

Chambers, R., (1997), *Where reality Counts ? Putting the First Last.* International Technology Publications, London.

Chambers, R., (1999), "Preface" (ed.) Shirly, K.While *The Art of Facilitating Participation*" New Delhi: Sage India.

Chandrasekhar, C.P., (2000), "Democratic Decentralisation and the Planning Principle. The Transition from below". Paper presented at the International Conference on Democratic Decentralisation, May 2000, State Planning Board, Kerala.

Cheema, G. and Rondinelli, (1983), *Decentralisation and Development: Policy Implementation in Developing Countries*, Sage, Landon.

Chenery, H. Ahluvalia, M. Bell, C. Duloy, R., (1974), *Redistribution with Growth.* New York: Oxford University Press.

Cohen and Peterson, (1999), *Administrative Decentralisation:* Kumerian Press, West Hartford.

Conyers, D., (1986), Future Directions in Development Studies: the case of Decentralisation. *World Development.* 14, pp. 593-603.

Cook, Bill, (1998), "Participation, Process and Management: Lessons for Development in the History of Organisational Development". *Journal of International Development,* 10(1) Jan- Feb 1998, pp. 35-54.

Cornie, Jolly, R. and Stewart, F., (1987), *Adjustment with a Human Face : Protecting the Vulnerable Promoting Growth*, Oxford; University Press.

CPGUKAN, (1991), "Community Participation for Health for All" Cited in Loenson, R., (1999). *Public Participation in Health Systems in Zimbabwe, Paper for accountability through Participation Workshop*, Brighton Institute of Development Studies.

Crook, Richard, C. and James, C.Mannuel, (1998), *Democracy and Decentralisation in South Asia and West Africa. Participation, Accountability and Performance.* Cambridge, 1998.

Dug Hindson and Bongani Ngqulunga, (2000), '*The Reconstruction of Local Government and the Evolution of Development Policy in Durban*'. Paper Presented at the

International Conference on Democratic Decentralisation, May 2000, State Planning Board, Kerala.

Dutta, Choudhari, M., (1989), "New Government Committed to Decentralisation" Economic Times, New Delhi, 13th December.

Ellickson, Robert, C., (1991), *Order without Law: How Neighbors Settle Disputes*, Harward University Press, Cambridge, Massachusetts.

Elson, D., (ed.), (1991), *Male Bias in the Development Process.* New York; Manchester University Press.

Emmerie, J., *(1991), Development Policies and the Crisis of the 1980s.* Paris Development Center for the OECD.

Escobar, A., (1995), *Encountering Development: The Making and Unmaking of the Third World*, Princeton: Princeton University Press.

Evans, Peter, (1995), *Embedded Autonomy: States and Industrial Transformation*, Princeton University Press, Princeton, NJ.

Evans, Peter, (1997), "Introduction. Development Strategies Across the Public and Private Divide In Evans, Peter (1997) *State Society Synergy. Governmental and Social Capital,* international and Area Studies, University of California, Berkely.

Fang Jing, (2000), "Participation : A Way to Better Health Outcomes ?" *IDS Bulletine.* Vol 31, No.1, January, 2000.

Fenster, T., (1993), "Settlement Planning and Participation Under Principles of Pluralism", *Progress in Planning*, 39, pp. 179-242.

Fleming, S., (1991), Between the House Hold : Researching Community Organisations and Networks, *IDS Bulletine*, 22, pp. 37-43.

Francois-Pirre Louis, (2000), *"Decentralisation and Democracy in Haiti"* Paper Presented at the International Conference on Democratic Decentralisation, May 2000, State Planning Board, Kerala.

Franke, R.W. Chasin, B.H., (1997), 'Power to the Malayalee People '*Economic and Political Weekly* Nov 29, pp. 3061-3068.

Freire, P., (1996), *Pedagogy of the Oppressed*, Penguin, London.

Gadgil, (1967), *District Development Planning.* Gokhale Institute of Planning and Economics.

Geisler, G., (1993), "Silences Speak Louder than Claims: Gender, Household and Agricultural Development in Southern Africa" *World Development*, 21, 1965-80, p. 2.

George Mathew, (1999), *"People's Plan : Kerala's Success Story", Kurukshethra,* Aug 1999, pp. 15-19.

Ghosh, Arun, (1988), "Popular Participation and Decentralised Planning in West Bengal" *Economic and Political Weekly,* 16th January.

Gibson–Graham, J.K., (1995), "Identity and Economic Plurality: Rethinking Capitalism and Capitalist Hegemony" *Environ-ment and Planning. Society and Space, 13, pp, 275-282.*

Gulati, I.S., (1994), *Panchyat Raj and Development,* Msgr. Thomas Nedumkallel Memorial Lecture, Msgr. Thomas Nedumkallel Memorial Committee, Nirmala College, Muvattupuzha.

Hahner, J., (1985), "Recent Research on Women in Brazil", *Latin American Research Review* 20, pp. 163-79.

Hans Blomkvist and Ashok Swain, (2001), Investigating Democracy and Social Capital in India', *Economic and Political Weekly,* Vol.XXXVI, Feb 24, 2001, pp. 639-645.

Hirshman, (1982), "The Rise and Decline of Development Economics" in Gersovitz.M, Diaz-Alejandro.C, Ranis, and Rosenwieg, M(Eds) The Theory and Experience of Economic Development: Essays in Honor of Sir.W.Arthur Lewis., Landon, Allen and Unwin, pp. 372-90.

Honderich, Ted, (1995), "The Question of Well Being and the Principle of Equality" *Mind, Oct.1981, 90,* pp. 481-504.

Huq, Mahabub Ul, (1976), *The Poverty Curtain: Choice for the Third World* , New York, Columbia University Press.

Hyden, (1997), "Civil Society, Social Capital and Development: Dissection of a Complex Discourse, Studies in Comparative International Development, 32,I, pp. 3-30.

Isaac, Thomas.T.M and Michael Tharakan, P.K., (1995), "Kerala: Towards a New Agenda" *Economic and Political Weekly* Aug 5-12, 1993-2004.

Isaac, Thomas, T.M., (1997), "People's Plan Campaign ; An interrim Assessment and Response to a Critique", in Chekkutty. N,P. (ed).

Isaac, Thomas.T.M., (1999), "The Socio Economic Political Context of Decentralised Planning Campaign' Paper Presented at the National Workshop on Decentralised Governance, KILA, Thrissur.

Isaac, Thomas T.M., (2000), *Local Democracy and Deveopment: Peoples Campaign for Decentralised Planning in Kerala.* Letword, Delhi.

Isaac, Thomas.T.M, Harilal, K.N.,(1997), Planning for Empowerment : People's Planning for Decentralised Planning in Kerala. *Economic & Political Weekly* Jan. 4-11, pp. 53-58.

Isaac, Thomas, T.M, Franke, W. Richard, (2000), *Local Democracy and Development : People's Campaign for Decentralised Planning in Kerala,* New Delhi: LeftWord.

Jenny Litrack and Seddon Jessica, (1999), "Decentralisation: Briefing Notes" World Bank Institute Working Papers. p. 3.

Jha, S.N., *Introduction, in* Jha, S.N., and Mathur, P.C., (1997), (Ed.) *Decentralisation and Local Politics: Readings in Indian Government and Politics" Sage, New -Delhi.1997.*

John, Brohman, (1996), *Popular Development, Rethinking the Theory and Practice of Development* Cambridge, Blackwell.

Jain, L.C., et.al, (1985), *Grass with out Roots,* Sage, New Delhi.

John Harris, (2000), *The Dialectics of Decentralisation: Comparing National Experiences.* Paper Presented at the International Conference on Democratic Decentralisation, May 2000, State Planning Board, Kerala.

John Kurian, (1997), 'On Development and Public Action: A Reflection on the Kerala Experience' in Sunil, Bastian and Nicola, Bastian, (Ed) (1997): *Assessing Participation: A debate from South Asia* Konark, New Delhi, 1997.

John, T. Milimo, (2000), 'Health Partnership in Zimbabwe', *IDS Bulletin,* Vol 31 Number 1, January 2000, Institute of Development Studies, Sussex, pp. 43-48.

Kambou, S.D., (1999), "How do we define participation? Are we ready to embrace it?" In: Embracing participation in development: worldwide experience from CARE's Reproductive Health Programs with a step-by-step field guide to participatory tools and techniques. Wisdom from the field, edited by Meera Kaul Shah, Sarah Degnan Kambou, Barbara Monahan. Atlanta, Georgia, CARE, Health and Population Unit, 1999 Oct. :1.1 - 1.10.

Karl, Marilee, (1995), *Women and Empowerment: Participation and Decision Making.* Zed Books, Landon.

Kaufman, Michael and Alfonso, Hafoldo Dilla, (1994), *Community Power and Grassroots Democracy: Transformation of Life.* Landon: Zed Books.

Keller, B. and Mbewe, D., (1991), Policy and planning for the empowerment of Zambia's women farmers, *Canadian Journal of Development Studies,* 12, pp. 75-88.

Khan, A., (1987), "A Comment on Professor Chakravarty's Paper" in Toye, J (ed) *Development Policies and the Crisis of the 1980s* Paris: Development Centre for the OECD, pp. 96-100.

Kirsten, Westergard, (1986), "Peoples Participation, Local Government and Rural Development", CDR Research Report. No.8, Copen Hagen; Centre for Development Research, 1986, p. 25.

Kitching, (1982), *Development and Underdevelopment in Historical Perspective: Populism, Nationalism and Industrialism,* New York: Methuen.

Kohen, M. and K. Deutsch, (1980), Decentralisation and Development : Policy Implementation in Developing Countries, Landon: Sage.

Kunhaman, M., (2000), People's Planning: Planning for a People's Paradigm" Paper presented at the International Conference on Democratic Decentralisation, May 2000, State Planning Board, Kerala.

Logan, K., (1990), 'Women's participation in urban protest'. in Foweraker, J and Craig, A. (eds). *Popular movements and political change in Mexico.*Boulder: Lynne Rienner, pp. 150-159.

Marschak, Thomas, (1959), "Centralisation and Decentralisation in Economic Organisation" *Econometrica,* Vol. 27(3), July.

Mayo, M. and G.Craig, (1995), "Community Participation and Empowerment: The Human face of Structural Adjustment Tools for Democratic transformation in G.Craig and M.Mayo (eds) Community Empowerment: A Reader in Participation and Development. London, Zed.

Loclan, E. and C. Mauffee, (1996), Hegemony and Socialist Strategy: Towards a Radical Democratic Politics, London, Verso.

Mahapatra, Bishnu, N., (2001), 'Social Connectedness and Fragility of Social Capital: View from an Orissa Village': *Economic and Political Weekly*, Vol. XXXVI, Feb 24, 2001. pp. 665-672.

Maro, P., (1990), 'The Impact of Decentralisation on Spatial Equity and Rural Development in Tanzania.' *World Development*, 18, pp. 673-693.

Martin, J., (1989), 'Mother Hood and Power : The Production of Women's Politics in a Mexican Community,' *American Ethnologist* 17, pp. 470-490.

Mathur, O.P., (1973), "Planning for Districts: Some Problems in Developing a Conceptual Frame Work" Prajnan. II, No. 3.

Mayer, Murkus, (2001), "Poverty, Local Planning and Youth Empowerment in Southern Sreelanka" Paper Presented at the International Conference on Democratic Decentralisation, May 2000, State Planning Board, Thiruvananthapuram, Kerala.

Mayo, M. and G.Craig, (1995), "Community Participation and Empowerment: The Human face of Structural Adjustment Tools for Democratic transformation in G.Craig and M.Mayo (eds) Community Empowerment: A Reader in Participation and Development. London, Zed.

Midgley, J., (1986), *Community Participation, Social Development and the State*, Landon: Mathuen.

Mohan, Giles and Kristian, Stokke, (2000), "Development and Empowerment: The Dangers of Localism" Paper presented at the International Conference on Democratic Decentralisation, May 2000, Trivandrum, Kerala.

Mohan, Giles, (1996), "Adjustment and Decentralisation in Ghana, A Case Study of Diminished Soveriegnity", *Political Geography, 15, 1*, pp. 75-94.

Molyneux, M., (1985), "Mobilisation without Emancipation ? Women's Interests, State and Revolution in Nicaragua" *Feminist Studies*, Vol. II, No. 2.

Moser, C., (1987), Mobilisation is Women's Work : Struggles for Infrastructure in Guayquil, Ecuador. IN Moser, C. and Peake, L. (eds) *Women, Human Settlements and Housing.* London: Tavistock, pp. 166-194.

Moser, C., (1989), "*Gender Planning in the Third World: Meeting Practical and Strategic Gender needs*", World Develop-ment, 17, pp. 1799-1825.

Mosse, D., (1995), "Authority, Gender and Knowledge. Theoretical Reflections on Participatory Rural Appraisal" *Economic and Political Weekly* March 18, pp. 569-578.

Mosse, D., (1997), "The Social Contradictions of People's Knowledge in Participatory Rural Development' in Sunil, Bastian and Nicola, Bastian, (Ed) : (1997) : *Assessing Participation: A debate from South Asia* Konark, New Delhi, 1997.

Mungai Lenneiye, (2000), "Testing Community Empowring Strategies in Zimbabwe: Examples from Nutrition Supplementation, Water Supply and Sanitation Programmes" *IDS Bulletin*, Vol. 31, Number 1, January 2000, Institute of Development Studies, Sussex, pp. 21-30.

Muraleedharan, K., (2000a), "Dynamics of Womens Participation in Development: The Kerala Experience" Paper presented at the Paper presented at the International Conference on Democratic Decentralisation, May 2000, State Planning Board, Kerala.

Muraleedharan, K., (2000b), "Womens Participation in Develop-ment : A Study of Dynamics of Women's Participation in the Local Level Planning of Kerala' *Asian Economic Review*, Vol. 42, August 2000, No. 2, pp. 338-353.

Muraleedharan, K., (2000c), "Participatory Planning in Kerala: Addressing some basic questions" Paper presented at 'Decentralised Planning : An Assessment;, the Workshop Organised by KRPLLD, CDS, Thiruvananthapuram, Kerala During October 2001.

Muraleedharan, K., (2001), "Women's Participation in Development and Capacity Builiding at Grass root Level : Some Observations from Kerala" IN S.P. Jain (Eds) *Emerging Institutions for Decentralised Developoment.* Vol II, NIRD, Hyderabad.

Muraleedharan, K., (2002), "Community Particpation in Decenra-lised Planning : Some Observations from Empirical Evidences" Paper presented at the 34th Annual Conference of Regional Science Conference held at Dr.John Mathai Center, Aranattukara, Thrissur, Kerala during Dec 25 to 26 2002.

Musgrave. R.A., (1959), *The theory of Public Finance,* Mac Graw Hill, New York.

Natraj, Lalitha, (1986), *An Analysis into Political Aspects of Planning in India, New Delhi: Inter India.*

Niraja Gopal Jayal, (2001), "Democracy and Social Capital in Central Himalaya : Tale of Two Villages" Economic and Political Weekly, Vol. XXXVI, Feb 24, 2001, pp. 655-664.

Nussbaum, Martha, (2003), "Gender and Governance : An Introduction" in Martha Nussbaum (Ed) *Essays on Gender and Governance*" HRDC, UNDP India. Source: WWW. UNDP. ORG. pub.

Oakely, P., et. al, (1991), *Projects with Peple: The Practice in Rural Development,* ILO, Geneva.

Oakely, R. and Marsdon, D., (1984), *Approaches to Participation in Rural Development,* ILO., Geneva.

Oates, E.W.,(1972), *Fiscal Federalism,* Harcount Brace Jouvanovich, New York.

Parpart, J., (1993), "Who is the 'other' ? A Post modern Feminist Critique of Women and Development Theory and Practice", *Development and Change,* 24, pp. 439-64.

Parpart, J., (2000), "Rethinking Participatory Empowerment, Gender and Development in a Global/Local World" Paper Presented at the Conference Organized by Center for Deve-loping-Area Studies, McGill University, 20-23 September 2000.

Patnaik, (2000), "Alternative Pardigms of Economic Decentrli-satioin "Paper presented at the International Conference on Democratic Decentralisation, May 2000, State Planning Board, Kerala.

Patrick Heller,(2000), "*Moving the State: The Politics of Decentralisation in Kerala,South Africa and Porto Alegre".* Paper Presented at the International Conference on Democratic Decentralisation, May 2000, State Planning Board, Kerala.

Paul, S., (1986), ***Community Participation in Development Projects-the World Bank Experiences*** : WB, Discussion Paper 6.

Paulo, Freire, (1996), Pedagogy of the Oppressed, Penguin, Landon.

Pearse, Andrews and Stiefel, Mathias, (1979), "Inquiry in to Participation : A Research Approach" *Popular Participation Programme,* The United Nations Research Institute for Social Development, (UNRISD): 1979, p. 5.

Pijnenburg, B. and Nhantumbo, I., (2002), *Participatory Development interventions in Mozambique.* Development in Practice. 2002 May;12(2):, pp. 192-9.

Pretty, J., et. al (1994), "Alternative Systems for Inquiry for a Sustainable Agriculture" IDS Bulletine, 25 (2).

Putnam, Robert, (1993), *Making Democracy Work: Civic Traditions in Modern italy,* Princeton, University Press.

Raj, K.N., (1971), "Planning from below with Reference to District Development and State Planning". *Economic and Political Weekly,* VI, Nos. 30-32.

Ralf, Strakloff, (1997), 'Participatory Discourses and Practice in a Water Resource Crisis in Sri Lanka' in Sunil, Bastian and Nicola, Bastian, (Ed) (1997): *Assessing Participation: A debate from South Asia* New Delhi, 1997.

Rajan Gurukkal, (2000), 'Coalition of Conflicting Interests and the Politics of Decentralisation: A Therectic Critique.' Paper Presented at the International Conference on Democratic Decentralisation, May 2000, State Planning Board, Kerala.

Radcliff, S and Westwood,S., (eds) (1996), *Women and Popular Protests in Latin America* New York :Routledge.

Renata, Serra, (2001), Social Capital: Meaningful and Measurable at the State Level', *Economic and Political Weekly,* Vol. XXXVI, Feb 24, 2001, pp. 693-695.

Rondinelli, D., McCullough, J., and R. Johnson, (1989), "Analys-ing Decentralisation Policies in Developing Countries: A Political-Economy framework" *Development and Change,* 20, pp. 57-87.

Rondinelli, D., Mucullough.J., and R. Johnson, (1989), "Analys-ing Decentralisation Policies in Developing Countries: A Political Economy Framework." *Deveopment and Change,* 20, pp. 57-87.

Rene Loewenson, (2000), "Public Participation in Health" *IDS Bulletin,* Vol. 31, No. 1, January 2000.

Sachidanandam, Shanti, (1997), 'Participatory Appraisal of Development under Civil War Conditions : The Experience of Batticaloa, Sree Lanka,1991-1995' in Sunil, Bastian and Nicola, Bastian, (Ed) (1997): *Assessing Participation: A Debate from South Asia* New Delhi, 1997.

Samaranayake, Mallika, (1997), "Significance of Participatory Approaches in Empowering People for Sustainable Development" in Sunil Bastian and Nicola, Bastian, (Ed) (1997) : *Assessing Participation: A debate from SouthAsia* Konark,New Delhi, 1997.

Samoff, J., (1990), "Decentralisation: the politics of interventionism". *Development and Change,* 21, pp. 513-530.

Simon, D. and Rakodi, C., (1990), Conclusions and Prospects : What Future for Regional Planning ? in Simon, D. (ed) : *Third Word Regional Development : A Reappraisal.* London; Chapman, pp. 249-260.

Singh, J.P. Vyas, N.N.Mann, R.S., (ed).(1988),*Tribal Women and Development* Rawat; Jaipur.

Slater, D.C., (1989), "Territorial Power and the Peripheral States: The Issue of Decentralisation" *Devleopment and Change,* 20, pp. 501-531.

Smith, (1995), *Decentralisation: The Territorial Dimension of State,* London, Allen and Unwin.

Stephen, L., (1989), *Not Just One of the Boys : From Female to Feminist in Popular Rural Movements in Mexico.* Paper Delivered at the Annual Meeting s of LASA (Latin American Studies Association): Pureto Rico.

Stokke, Kristian, (1998), "Globalisation and the Politics of Poverty alleviation in the South." Norvegean Journal of Geography, 52, pp. 221-228.

Stohr, W., (1981), *Development from Below: The Bottom-up and Periphery-inward Development Paradigm.* Chichester; Wiley.

Stohr and Tailor, D., (eds) (1981), *Development from Above or Below ? The Dialectics of Regional Planning in Developing Countries* Chichester: Wiley.

Stirrat, R.L., (1997), "The New Orthodoxy and Truths: Participa-tion, Empowerment and other Buzz Words" in Sunil, Bastian and Nicola, Bastian, (Ed) (1997): *Assessing Partici-pation: A debate from South Asia* ,New Delhi.

Sudha, Pai, (2001), "Social Capital, Panchayaths and Grass Roots Demcocracy: Politics of Dalit Assertion in Uttarpradesh". Economic and Political Weekly, Vol. XXXVI, Feb 24, 2001. pp. 646-654.

Sutton, P., (1989), *Development Ideology, its Emergence and Decline*, Deadulus, 118, pp. 35-67.

Turner, Mark and Hulme, David, (1997), "Governance, Adminis-tration and Development. Making the Sate Work. 1997, Kumerian Press, West Hartford, p. 159.

Vettivel, S.K., (1999), *Particpation: Concept, Approaches and Techniques, New Delhi, Vetri, New Delhi.*

United Nations, (1981), Popular Participation as a Strategy for Promoting Country Level action and Natural Development, New York, UNP.

Uphoff, Norman, T. and Cohen, John. *Rural Development Participation : Concepts and Measures for Project Design Implementation and Evaluation,* Ithaca: Cornell University, 1977.

Vengroff, R. and Johnston, A., (1989), 'Decentralisation and the Implementation of Rural Development' in Senegal: *The View from Below*. New York: Edwin Mellen.

Wignaraja, P., (1991), "Genesis of Intellectual Quest: An Over-view", Wignaraja, P, Hussain, A. Sethi, H., Wignaraja, G. (Co Authors) *Participatory Development : Learning from South Asia*, Oxford University Press.

William Tordoff, (1994), "Decentralisation, Comparative Experience in Common Wealth Africa, Journal of Modern African Studies, Vol. 32, No. 4, pp. 555-580.

World Bank, (1990), "Strengthening Local Governments in Sub Saharan Africa" EDI Policy Seminar. Report Series 21, Washington D.C, WB.

World Bank, (1997), *World Development Report : The State in a Changing World*, Oxford, Oxford University Press.

Zesuliwe Mkhize, (2000), "Decentralisation: A Grassroots Pers-pective." Paper presented at the International Conference on Democratic Decentralisation, May 2000, State Planning Board, Kerala.

2

Concepts, Definitions and Methodology

PARTICIPATION : THEMES AND CONCEPTS

Inspite of the wide acceptability of Participation as a development strategy, as a concept it is still defined and interpreted in a multitude of ways. A preliminary understanding about the concepts will serve to provide the right perspective of the process and dynamics involved in it. This chapter serves the purpose of examining these concepts from a critical approach. A detailed note on the methodology, the sample the data and the required profile of sample and sample of households are also provided as it is essential for a fair appreciation of issue under discussion.

As far as the discussion of the core concept of participation is concerned, it may be helpful to begin with some critical remarks. As observed by several authors, Participation is an illusive concept, in both literature and field. (Bastian 1997: Kambou S.D 1999: Pijnenburg.B and Nhantumbo. I 2002) sometimes it is promoted as a very new approach different from those that have dominated in developing countries. At some other times, participation is used as a method to get the

projects implement. (Wignaraja 1991; Bhatnagar 1992). Bastian (1997) sketches four different thematic variations in the concept of participation in his attempts 'to identify the principal characteristics, ideological frameworks and politics of what goes on as participation'.

First, Participation is employed as a simple means to getting unpaid labour from the people. The strong argument behind this variant of participation is that it serves the purpose of creating a sense of belonging among the public about the public utilities created. From the corners of policy makers and planners with strong bias towards reducing the burden of welfare expenditures, this practice has drawn strong support. In other words , it is a simple technique to get the free labour of the poor for the development projects. Apart from the free labour they contribute, this variant involves hardly any involvement by the people in development.

Second, Participation is often interpreted as an attempt to promote self-reliance. Those who support this variant of participation mostly share some common ideological strands like the poor in the third world apparently lack any initiative for their betterment and the poverty they are suffering is the direct outcome of this character, rather than that of the concrete-socio economic structures they are trapped in. They also share the belief that the poor countries in the third world depend on the developed world to a large extent and 'this structural explanations of dependency at the macro level is being transformed to the situations in the micro level'.

Third, Participatory approach is often resorted as a technique to create ideal villages. This approach has the vision of a harmonious village of the past, where everybody lived peacefully and solved problems together. This is the most popular version of participation and the most criticized one.

Finally, Participation is also resorted as a method of Project Management. It is believed that by adopting participatory methods project can be successfully managed and completed. Bastian's sarcastic remarks conclude that this type of participatory approach is the 'growth sector of participatory industry' as variety of methods is being evolved and many organizations have emerged to develop and market these methodologies.

Chambers (1995) feels that Participation, as a concept, has experienced a renaissance in the 70s and he identifies three main ways in which participation is used in the context of development. First, it is used, as a cosmetic label to make whatever is proposed appears as good. Second, it is used as a method for co-opting local labour to reduce the cost of maintenance of projects. Thirdly, it is a way of empowering people by enabling them to take decisions on the problems they encounter and the possible ways of getting out of them.

Samaranayake (1997), while elaborating her field experiences, agrees with Chambers cosmetic label theory. Several experts and development workers have cited such kind of stories in which participation is made a cosmetic label to make everything done appear good and appreciating. In a few cases, participation is confined to simply attending the Grama Sabhas or such kind of meetings and signing the attendance sheets for ratifying the decisions taken by outside experts. Claims will be made that discussions are made with the local people and it is portrayed as true participation. It is true that, in this context, there is no genuine participation and what actually happens is simple ratification of the proceedings. Hence, these may be called ratification meetings and not Participation. Some of the informants we met for the household survey conducted in connection with the research project re called that there are several people, due to some external pressures for nominal participation, merely come to the halls and leaves after signing the registers. However, for reasons unknown, we rarely had such experiences during our exposures to Grama Sabha meetings in Kerala, particularly in the sample area. Midgley (1986) calls this kind of participation as 'Pseudo participation' and the other one as 'Authentic Participation' in which local people directly controls the resources and exerts their voice in decision-making.

Participation is in its ideal form when there is self-organization, self-responsibility and self-actualization, says Burkey (1993). He opines that participation is an essential part of human growth, development of self-confidence, pride, initiative, creativity, responsibility and co-operation. In this approach, people learn to take charge of their own lives and find solution to their own problems and the essence of development being built by such kind of participation will be sustainable.

Distinguishing between Coerced Participation, Induced Participation and Spontaneous Participation, United Nations (1981) condemns Coerced Participation, regards Induced Participation as the second best and as far as Spontaneous Participation (or Bottom up Participation) is concerned, it believes that Spontaneous Participation (or Bottom up Participation) comes closer to the ideal mode of Participation as it reflects voluntary and autonomous action on the part of the people to organise and deal with their problems.

Participation can be identified based on the aims of it according to Conyers (1985). It can be either for improving project results or for participation itself. In agreement with the first line of argument, he defines participation as a means to improve the quality and relevance of projects by facilitating their implementation, including the contribution and acceptance of local resources. UNCHS (1984) also assent with this, when it states that People's participation is the execution of projects by contributing their ingenuity, skills and other untapped resources. More people can benefit if implementation is facilitated with popular participation and outcome responds better to the needs and priorities of the beneficiaries. The second line of argument goes on defining Participation as an end itself, as an essential component of a democratic society to ensure the well-being of individuals and communities. (Conyers, 1985). Moser (1989) is of the opinion that Participation, at the outset, in decision-making is a precondition of the objective of empowerment. Where Participation is a means to achieve a development objective, it is usually included only at the implementation and maintenance level.

Participation is viewed, by Paul (1993) as an active process by which beneficiaries influence the directions and execution of a development project with a view to enhancing their well being in terms of income, personal growth, self reliance or other values as they cherish. Fenster (1993), in accord with the United Nations, views participation in its diametrical forms like Spontaneous Participation or Bottom up Participation, and Induced Participation or Top down Participation or Coerced Participation.

When Oakely and Marsdon (1984) observe that these common interpretations of participation may be represented as a continuum, they are really reiterating what Bastian has stated. Participation, at one extreme end, may assume the nature of voluntary contribution towards the implementation of the development projects with particularly no influence over its shape. At the other end, it may assume the form of active and decisive participation to increase local or community's control.

People's Participation evolve around three pivotal points such as 1) Effective networking in the village for dissemination of information. 2) Equal opportunity for all people in the village for expressing their opinion and 3) Institutional support for implementation of projects, according to UNIDS (1977). Another aspect of Participation highlighted by UNIDS is that it is closely related to the level of economic development attained by the society. There is a positive correlation between these variables. At low level of development participation will be confined to the elites of the community, which in turn will lead to manipulation of participation, the majority being literally too poor to participate. In other words, when there is much poverty and misery in the local economy, there may not be much incentive to participate. There fore, the first attempt should be to increase the divisible surplus of the community, so that the worse section will get the due share in the surplus and this will act as a motive for participation. Participation, thus, follow closely the pace of economic development.

Participation is meaningless unless active, observes Lalitha Nataraj (1986). Popular Participation, as a process, can be defined as active and meaningful involvement of the mass of people at different level. First, in the decision making process for the determination of social goals and allocation of resources to achieve them, and second, in the voluntary execution of resulting projects and programmes.

Popular participation, according to World Employment Programme of the ILO, (ILO, 1978) can contribute to basic needs strategy by playing a part in

the definition of basic needs, by enhancing the generation of resources to meet basic needs, by improving the distribution of goods and services and by satisfying the psychological desire to participate in decision making which affect their lives. But this approach misses the pivot of the problem, as it stress on the institutional aspect of power and leaves out the need for structural change and shift in power relations.

Participation, according to United Nations Research Institute for Social Development (1979), is a means of particularly those currently without power, to redistribute both the control of resources and power, in favor of those live by their own productive labour. In other words, participation is a collective effort to increase and exercise control over resources and institutions on the part of groups and movements of those hither to get excluded from control. (Westergaard, 1986).

Participation or empowerment is both a goal and method of change. As a goal, it refers to a society where hardly there is monopoly of the means of political power, economic, cultural and social power in the hands of particular class, sex, social stratum or bureaucratic elite. As a means and method of change, participation is a means to develop the views and organisational capacity of those presently excluded, it is also a means for the majority of population to identify and express their needs and to contribute directly to the solving of social problems. (Kaufman and Alfonso, 1994).

Inspite of the disagreement on various aspects of participation, like meaning and definition, most of the analysts emphasise on the decision-making role of community as an essential and ingredient of Participation. (Fleming, 1991). As Cornie (Cornie, et al, 1987) observed, such participation, where there is a

voice in crucial decisions, helps to influence the design of policies, so that they correspond to the needs and conditions of the people. Participation is also defined as sharing of the benefit of projects, as development economist view it, and as community's contribution to decision-making as Social planners view it (Fenster, 1993).

EXPERIENCE SHARING

It may also be useful and interesting to look, in the case of Participatory Approach to Development, what the theory misses, how the critics have interpreted it, as well as, how far what one see in the fields are distant from what the theory holds. The literature is flooded with such attempts and experience sharing. It seems quite logical to classify the work so far done as falling in to two broad categories critical assessment and experience sharing, than resorting to a spatial or chronological classification of any type as followed in most of the research works. This section attempts to sketch some of the serious critical comments on it and share some experiences of experts and practitioners of this approach across the globe.

Perhaps the most serious and contributive criticism of Participatory Approach came from Stirrat(1997). He attacks the basic scaffoldings and supporting pillars of this approach. Participatory approach to development has become orthodoxy in development strategy and almost all of the projects and programmes essentially bear a participatory component in it currently, says Stirrat.(1997). Unfortunately, 'hardly there is a single definition of this orthodoxy and what exists is a set of loosely connected ideas and approaches, developed in response to what its proponents see as an older misguided orthodoxy of development'. Consequently, we have a rather eclectic as well as theoretically confused approach to participation in development. Though what ever has been written about this approach attained canonical status, the interpretations about them are confusing. Interpretations have added more confusion than clarity to the theme, the approach, and the practical aspects.

What lies at the root of the new orthodoxy is the strong skepticism about the role the State, the bureaucracy, and western technical forms of knowledge do play in the development industry. Paradoxically, while it is all set to criticise the forms of western technical forms of knowledge, it seeks its legitimating in the forms of populist rhetoric, says Stirrat.

One of the striking and most prominent features of the new orthodoxy is the sharing of common vocabulary like 'village', 'community', 'the poor', 'participation' and 'empowerment'. All these collectively picture a rural society, which existed outside time and history. This picturisation of rural society has been derived' from the Victorian ideas about the European past, and an imperial idea that "Oriental present represented European past". To put it differently, at the basic scaffolding of this approach lies the imaginary non-existing form of rural life. The term 'Organic Communities' frequently appears in the literature of this approach again places one in the land of imagination and fantasy. The community portrayed in this literature is harmonious and ideal in which the villagers' co operate with each other, and Stirrat calls it as the "nostalgic views of the English rural past imposed on the South Asian rural present". The problems lies in the fact that 'villages cannot be treated as single entity, at least from sociological point of view, cheerful co-operation is rarely existent, villagers hardly act as a single unit'. Apart from this, the imaginary village concept, the local people or rural people who are supposed to inhabit in this villages, in reality, are far distant from what is conceived in theory. The people are represented as sharing common interests, against what we experienced in our visits to Grama Sabhas and Ayalkootams, where they stand for varied, conflicting interests according to their age, gender, kinship, class, caste, and off course political association. Against the real picture of conflicting interests often in continuous clash with each other, the villages and the complexity of the rural life is being disguised denying any room of historical change.

In his attempt to provide a theoretical critique to the 'coalition of conflicting interests in the Politics of decentralization', Rajan Gurukkal (2000) has picturised the present reality in Kerala in the context of efforts for introducing participatory approach and decentralization. Kerala is a microcosm of India, with few distinctive features like high literacy, extensive health care facilities, better communication and transport infrastructure and the socio-economic situation of Kerala is characterised by the competitive co-existence of diverse groups, mainly of the middle class with a relatively low percentages of higher income groups placed above and huge number of tribes, scheduled castes and other backward classes placed below. These groups, according to Gurukkal, are increasingly resorting to the politics of caste, religion and ethnic identities cutting across the class difference for gaining power and resource control.

Starkloff (1997) is of the opinion that participatory discourses in general fail to problematise the fact that ' the people' always participate in development in one form or the other, either as beneficiaries of projects or those employed to implement the projects. All these constitute participation though they do hardly involve in decision-making, or are not mobilsed by the 'community mobiliser' as perceived in the participatory programmes. The orthodoxy of participation, as it employ a highly selective and often narrow meaning of participation, fails to recognize participation as an open network of power relations. The fact is that participation is more complex than most of the participatory development projects can cope with.

An important ingredient of participatory planning is the access to local knowledge and its use in development exercises. In his attempt to examine some of the conceptual and practical issues associated with this new focus on 'people's knowledge' and 'local knowledge' into planning systems, David Mosse (1997) argues that 'people's knowledge' is widely misconceived as a discrete and autonomous category within externally controlled planning systems. As conceived in the assumptions, the contention that local knowledge and its access can hardly transform bureaucratic planning, is baseless as it fails to look at local knowledge as a product of social relations, and views it as a fixed commodity. What is reflected as local knowledge or people's knowledge is itself constructed in the context of planning and reflects social relationships. The fact is that the new forms of local knowledge are subordinated to established forms of planning which often weakens the chances of participatory techniques effecting shifts towards decentralization or participation in rural development administration.

He suggests that participatory pogrammes have to focus critical attention on the social construction of participatory planning. This is as important as acquiring a set of participatory planning techniques and a pre requisite for their effective use. According to him, the issues facing participation is not confined to the capacity of public systems to adopt these approaches One important issue is concerned with the generation of local knowledge which will be limited by the programme policies. Even in case of projects, which are supposed, to be implemented by using participatory techniques, administrative control will be asserted in the production of local knowledge. Secondly, but more serious, is the danger of curtailing of knowledge within projects, because of the mutually reinforcing interac-tions between programme policy and 'local knowledge'.

Recently, partly in response to the emerging crisis in health care provisions in many countries, there has been a major shift in attitude towards community interaction. Approaches, which viewed communities as passive recipients of health care, have given way to those that seek to make more of the potential of active participation for enhanced accountability and improved responsiveness of services. Several attempts in this regard can be traced across the globe. The success ratings and failures reports raise several questions of theoretical and empirical importance. Andrea Cornwell, Henry Lucas and Kith Pastener (2000) make such an attempt to examine the above aspects. As they feel any analysis of participatory framework for development has to go beyond "assumptions about a homogeneous community to consider the contested dynamics of intra-community relations, especially in terms of gender". In focusing on the interface between communities and providers, issue of differences between communities cannot be overlooked. As the authors assert, any participatory framework has to address the questions about issues of equity at the local level and mechanisms that might promote more equitable engagement with community based initiatives. Explicit attentions to the issues of difference is needed as the increasing community control over priority setting and resource management can all too easily entrench the exclusion of marginal groups and their particular health needs.

Rone Loewenson (2000), while sharing the varied experience of Zimbabe in public participation in health care systems, argues that participation is an end in itself, building networks of solidarity in social groups, building institutional capacity and empowering people to understand and influence the decisions that affect their lives. Despite the widely accepted fact that participation can play a vital role in enhancing the quality of health services delivery, it is hardly implemen-ted and evaluated while planning is made in the health sector. According to the authors, the barriers of effective public participation in health sector are (1) the inertia of conventional planning and top down process of expert identification of problems and solutions merely haunt the process of participation. (2) The lack of cohesion, organizational structures and capacities for effective participation stand in the way. (3) Community inputs may be discouraged by the paternalistic attitude of health workers and mystified nature of health information. Finally, (4) the bureaucratisation of health care often distance people and communities from it.

The author has also looked in to the circumstances, which pressed for more participation in health services, and provide a profile of the process of participatory interventions by the community in health activities. The paradigm shift from redistributive and more equity oriented health policies towards and market oriented reforms have reduced real per capita budget allocation and increased pressure on household finance to meet health needs. The policy review within health sector has worked a strong motivating factor for different groups to seek greater influence on decision making in health.

The decentralization policies, increased community contributions, demand for increased role of communities in decision-making and resource utilisation have enhanced participation of different groups in this health activities. Formerly, public participation in health was confined to the governance of health activities and was not extended to the choice and negotiations made in this sector. Health issue began to take up jointly than individually and the people began to prefer for more collective mechanisms, which in turn prepared the structure for effective participation.

The study concludes that, in Zimbabwe, great concern has been shown across all communities for participation as well as accountability. This has called for strengthened joint mechanisms involving civic and elected leaders and health providers, with clear terms of reference, roles, authorities, adequate training, and resource for their functioning. There is strong evidence for the positive contribution of public participation in health and the need for it is supported and enhanced.

Lenneiye (2000) attempts to examine the evolution of development structures responsible for nutrition and water supply, how community participation operates within these structures at different phases and the lessons learned from these in Zimbabwe. Community involvement is feasible where the external agencies primarily drive development initiatives and invite communities to become involved. The term participation is appropriate when the external agents seeks a partnership with communities, but retains control by the community. By community empowerment, it is understood that resources are controlled by communities through their elected structures, and it is these structures that define the terms under which external agencies can become involved. As far as the

benefits of participation are concerned, the author is highly optimistic. There has been a steady taking back of power over resources by local bodies in Zimbabwe. Inspite of all these difficulties, the community groups involved in Child Supplementary Feeding Programme (CSFP) and Integrated Rural Water Supply and Sanitation Programme (IRWSSP) were able to gain useful organizational skills that have been extended to other areas also.

Wilkies (2000) has provided a detailed analysis of issues concerning participation at micro level, and examines the influences that different interests have, the different channels for voicing interests and unequal power relations place on the outcomes of decision-making process. As the author feels, Participation is said to be of a high degree when communities identify their potential and mobilize to carry out their own plans against the lesser degree of participation such as consultation, delegation or passive participation.' (CPGUKAN 1991: Pretty et. al 1994) Citing the experience of Laba village, China the study arrives at the conclusion that, it is possible for the village to be making all the decisions regarding the health scheme and the transition cost can be significantly reduced by initiating and implementing the scheme through dominant power structures. Evaluation of the schemes found that accountability could not be enforced due to the peculiar structures and processes, and there has not been a marginal group with unmet needs. The voice of the marginal groups can be heard and made influential on the outcome of the decision making process, if the external actors have a profound effect on the marginal groups. The study attempts to trace out what goes on inside the process of participation and decision-making. Participation in decision making can be understood as a process involving both 'voice' and 'influence'. Voice,

as the author observes, is the ability to share knowledge or opinion relevant to a certain decision. Voice can improve certain technical quality of some decisions and potentially improve the fairness of interest related decisions. Influence is viewed as a capacity to contribute effectively to the outcome of a decision making process in order to secure ones interests. In this background, the study concludes that having voice is hardly a sufficient condition for influencing decision making due to the fact that the outcome of the decision making process is influenced more by the relative power and interests. What this suggests that it needs to deconstruct the popular assumption of homogeneity of the community and more attention is paid to power relations between groups within the community. This suggestion is highly contributive towards the efforts of sustaining participation.

Fang Jing (2000) attempts to examine what participation means, how it can happen, what advantages it can bring and what constraints it faces, and finally its future in China in the present development context.

Crook and Mannuel (1998) have attempted to investigate three specific questions related to Participation such as; how had patterns of political participation has changed as a result of decentralised planning, how had the performance of government institutions changed, and finally, were changes in participation and changes in institutional performance interrelated. The study has taken in to account the experiences of four countries viz., India, Ghana, Bangladesh and Cote d, Ivoire. However, the participation, in this paper, is approached from a very narrow point of view and confined to political participation alone.

Participatory approach to development and decentralization attempts can be viewed from the perspective of Social Capital formation also (Isaac 2000; Ellikson 1997; Evans 1991). Ever since Robert Putnam (1993) has analysed the impact of social capital on the functioning of local level institutions in Italy, the concept has captured scholarly attention worldwide. (Pai 2001). Blomkvist and Swain (2001) observe that social capital refers to the trust, network and norms shared by a group of actors that enable them to act upon together more efficiently to pursue their goals and shared objectives. Though the concept has been with us even as early as 1916, it has taken more than four decades to understand and establish the fact that citizen's experience and knowledge have an impact on the economic development. The credit for shifting the debate about the prerequisites of development and democracy from ideology and institutions to cultural factors such as value and virtue goes to Putnam.

A few recent attempts to examine various aspects of Social Capital in the context of democratic decentralization and grass roots democracy can be traced. (Sudha Pai; Bhomkvist and Swain; Niraja Gopal and Jayal; Mahapatra; Bhattacharya; Mayer; Renata Serra 2001) According to Blomkvist and Swain, the theoretical significance of the study of Social Capital will focus attention on non-material resources at the micro level and their possible impact at the macro level. The essential questions need to be asked are how far these resources are structured based on class, caste, religious group or spatial belonging. The study of Blomkvist and Swain focused in Orissa examines the protest mobilizations in India. Orissa, during the post independence period, has been poles apart in political and economic movements and the coastal regions have more powerful movements compared to inland. Apart from this, the environmental movements in inland Orissa have been weaker compared to the coastal counterparts.

This has been due to the failure to gather momentum because the different groups failed come together. It is inferred, by the author, that some times strong communal bonding social capital becomes a hindrance to coming together for a common cause.

Sudha Pai has attempted to analyse the impact of social capital on the democratic functioning of the two districts of Uttar Pradesh. The study has clearly shown that segmentation arising out of caste class divisions of the society emerges as an important significant contextual variable that tends to determine the development of trust and social capital between different groups and the functioning of democratic institutions. Since independence, there has been increased differentiation and not homogenisation. Social capital is not confined to upper and dominant class but has sharpened between sections of the poor and marginalized. The study has identified the formation of social capital within and segments in rural society. It is individual identities rather than group identities that create social capital reservoirs within segments, and this hinder the creation of constructive social capital, which can contribute towards effective functioning of democratic governments. Rarely there is trust among the individuals as the members of Panchayat or community sharing common interest except in the case of common crisis or a programme that benefits all like roads and bridges. Sudha Pai observes that the incapacity of the Social Capital to cut across the boundaries has hindered collective action among all castes and groups especially the rural poor, greater participation and democratic functioning of the Panchayats. Unlike in Western countries, where the emphasise is on the equal citizen's participation in public life for the common good, in these Panchayats unequal relations of power, competition and conflict occupy the center place. This observation of

Sudha Pai clearly sees eye to eye, with what we have experienced in our participation sessions in the Kaiparamab and Porkalam Grama Panchayats. Most of the key resource persons, leaders as well as other engineers of the programme were highly apprehensive about the inter-group and intra-group conflicts that often fetter participation in the process of planning. Sudha pai, still shares a bright and optimistic feeling that a broad based social capital capable of bringing together different caste, class groups may evolve over a period of time and an interplay of both conflict and consensus, negotiation and bargaining, leading to more democratic functioning of Panchayats.

Niraja Gopal Jayal (2001) hardly shares the apprehensions raised by Sudha Pai and in a study of the link between democracy and social capital in the context of rural hill society in the Central Himalayas, the author observes that social homogeneity does not necessarily or invariably issue in powerful reserves of social capital.

THE METHODOLOGY AND SAMPLE

This work is an outcome of a couple of research projects[1] done by the author in the area of Participatory development and Women Empowerment in the background of participatory planning in Kerala, supported by external agencies like Ministry of External Affairs, Government of Netherlands and Sunya Foundation respectively. The major source of information is primary data collected through (i) household survey conducted with semi-structured questionnaire and (ii) participant observations and focus group discussions. All available adult members in the sample area were interviewed using different set of questionnaires. As a supplementary source of information, the leaders and officials actively engaged in local level planning were also interviewed with another set of questionnaire.

The basic unit of the study is the households in the grama panchayats. Multi- stage sampling technique was used for selecting the sample households. There are 14 districts in Kerala State. Thrissur district has contributed the largest number of Women Panchayat Members and Women Presidents during the last term of local bodies. There are 38 Women Panchayat Presidents and 199 women Panchayat Members in Thrissur district. Hence, Thrissur district was selected in the first stage, as the sample district, since the research projects were from gender perspective of participation.

There are 98 Grama Panchayats and 7 Municipalities in Thrissur district. Selection of grama panchayats is made based on quantity of participation. In the second stage, from these 98 Grama Panchayats, two Grama Panchayats were selected: *Kaiparamb Grama Panchayat of Puzhakkal Development Block* with largest participation and *Porkalam Grama Panchayat of Chovannur Development Block* with lowest participation were selected.

In the third stage, Grama Panchayat wards were selected based on rate of people's participation in Grama Sabhas. Two Grama Panchayat wards, one with largest participation and the other with lowest participation, each from these Grama Panchayats were selected for an intensive study at the household level. In Kaiparamb Grama Panchayat the study was conducted at ward No. 2, the ward with better participation and ward No 8, ward with poor participation. Similarly, in Porkalm Grama Panchayat, ward No. 8 with better participation and ward 2, with poor participation, were selected for the study.

In the fourth and final stage, sample households were selected using Systematic Random Sampling Method. There were 500- 600 households in the selected wards. From each ward, a sample of 100 houses was selected randomly. In order to avoid clustering of sample units in same area, and to ensure representation of all the areas, systematic random sampling was adopted and every sixth house was selected, skipping the houses in between them. This has helped to get the sample units spread throughout the population area in the wards and the responses obtained were more representative. In this manner sample of around 125 and odd households from each wards of two Grama Panchayats were identified and from each house available elders were interviewed using a semi structured questionnaire. As a whole there were 500 and odd households informants in the sample. Participant observations and focus group discussions were held for supplementing and substantiating the information gathered through house hold survey.

NOTE

1. The research projects were broadly in the area of Participatory Planning in Kerala and specifically in the area of Dynamics of Women's Participation and Empowerment of Women. The first project, which has been supported by Ministry of External Affairs, Government of Netherlands and Kerala Research Programme on Local Level Development, Center for Development Studies, Thiruvanan-thapuram, Kerala has looked in to the basic questions of participation like who participates, how and for what they participate. Besides, it has examined the perspective of non-participants also. The second research project, supported by Sunya Foundation, Gujarat has examined the empowerment process of women in the background of participatory planning in Kerala and revealed the micro level realities of empowerment process. It has also examined the impact of empowerment exercises in Kerala.

REFERENCES

Andrea Cornwall, Hentry Lucas and Kath Pasteur, (2000), Accountability Through Participation: Developing Workable Partnership models in Health Sector'. *IDS Bulletin*, Vol. 31, Number 1, January 2000, Institute of Development Studies, Sussex, pp. 1-14.

Andrea Wilkes, (2000), *"The Function of Participation in a Village Based Health Repayment Scheme : What can Participation Actually do?" IDS Bulletin*, Vol. 31, No. 1, January 2000, Institute of Development Studies, Sussex, pp. 31-36.

Bastian, Sunil and Bastian, Nicola, (Ed.), (1997), *Assessing Participation : A debate from South Asia*, New Delhi.

Bhattacharya, Dwaipayan, (2001), "Human Development and Civic Community in India : Making Democracy Perform" *Economic and Political Weekly*, Vol. XXXVI, Feb 24, 2001, pp. 673-684.

Bhatnagar, B. and Williams, (1992), (ed.) "*Participatory Development and the World Bank, Potential Directions for Change*", World Bank Discussion Papers, No. 183, October 1992.

Burkey, S., (1993), *People First, A Guide to Self Reliant Participatory Rural Development*, London : Zed Books, Landon.

Chambers, R., (1995), "*Paradigm Shifts and the Practice of Participatory Development", Nelson. S and Wright. S Power and Participatory Development : Theory and Practice*. Intermediate Technology Publications, London.

Conyers, D., (1986), Future Directions in Development Studies: the Case of Decentralisation. *World Development*, 14, pp. 593-603.

Cornie, Jolly, R. and Stewart, F., (1987), *Adjustment with a Human Face : Protecting the Vulnerable Promoting Growth*, Oxford; University Press.

CPGUKAN, (1991), "Community Participation for Health for All" cited in Loenson, R., (1999) Public Participation inHealth Systems in Zimbabwe, Paper for Accountability through *Participation Workshop*, Brighton Institute of Development Studies.

Crook, Richard, C. and James, C. Mannuel, (1998), *Democracy and Decentralisation in South Asia and West Africa. Participation, Accountability and Performance.* Cambridge, 1998.

Ellickson, Robert, C., (1991), *Order without Law: How Neighbors Settle Disputes*, Harward University Press, Cambridge, Massachusetts.

Evans, Peter, (1995), *Embedded Autonomy: States and Industrial Transformation*, Princeton University Press, Princeton.

Fang Jing, (2000), "Participation : A Way to Better Health Outcomes ?" *IDS Bulletine.* Vol. 31, No. 1, January 2000.

Fenster, T., (1993), "Settlement Planning and Participation under Principles of Pluralism", *Progress in Planning*, 39, pp. 179-242.

Isaac, Thomas, T.M., (2000), *Local Democracy and Deveopment: Peoples'Campaign for Decentralised Planning in Kerala.* Leftword, Delhi.

Kambou, S.D., (1999), "How do we Define Participation? Are we Ready to Embrace it?" In : Embracing Participation in Development: Worldwide Experience from CARE's Reproductive Health Programs with a Step-by-step Field Guide to Participatory Tools and Techniques. Wisdom from the Field, Edited by Meera Kaul Shah, Sarah Degnan Kambou, Barbara Monahan. Atlanta, Georgia, CARE, Health and Population Unit, 1999 Oct.: 1.1-1.10.

Kaufman, Michael and Alfonso, Hafoldo Dilla, (1994), *Community Power and Grassroots Democracy: Transformation of Life.* Landon: Zed Books.

Midgley, J., (1986), *Community Participation, Social Development and the State*, Landon: Mathuen.

Moser, C., (1989), "*Gender Planning in the Third World : Meeting Practical and Strategic Gender Needs*", World Development, 17, pp. 1799-1825.

Mosse, D., (1995), "Authority, Gender and Knowledge. Theoreti-cal Reflections on Participatory Rural Appraisal" *Economic and Political Weekly* March 18, pp. 569-578.

Mosse, D., (1997), "The Social Contradictions of People's Knowledge in Participatory Rural Development' in Sunil,

Bastian and Nicola, Bastian, (Ed): (1997): *Assessing Participation: A debate from South Asia* Konark ,New Delhi, 1997.

Mungai Lenneiye, (2000), 'Testing Community Empowring Strategies in Zimbabwe: Examples from Nutrition Supplementation, Water Supply and Sanitation Programmes' *IDS Bulletin*, Vol. 31, Number 1, January 2000, Institute of Development Studies, Sussex, pp. 21-30.

Mahapatra, Bishnu, N., (2001), 'Social Connectedness and Fragi-lity of Social Capital: View from an Orissa Village': *Economic and Political Weekly*, Vol. XXXVI, Feb 24, 2001, p. 665.

Mayer, Murkus, (2001), "Poverty, Local Planning and Youth Empowerment in Southern Sree lanka" Paper presented at the International Conference on Democratic Decentralisation, May 2000, State Planning Board, Thiruvananthapuram, Kerala.

Natraj, Lalitha, (1986), *An Analysis into Political Aspects of Planning in India, New Delhi: Inter India.*

Niraja Gopal Jayal, (2001), "Democracy and Social Capital in Central Himalaya : Tale of Two Villages" Economic and Political Weekly, Vol. XXXVI, Feb 24, 2001, pp. 655-664.

Oakely, R. and Marsdon, D., (1984), *Approaches to Participation in Rural Development*, ILO., Geneva.

Paul, E., (1993), "Prospectus for Liberalisation in Singapore", *Journal of Contemprory Asia*, 23, pp. 1871-5.

Pearse, Andrews and Stiefel, Mathias, (1979), "Inquiry in to Participation: A Research Approach" *Popular Participation Programme*, The United Nations Research Institute for Social Development, (UNRISD): 1979, p. 5.

Pijnenburg, B. and Nhantumbo, I., (2002), *Participatory development interventions in Mozambique*. Development in Practice, 2002 May; 12 (2), pp. 192-9.

Putnam, Robert, (1993), *Making Democracy Work: Civic Traditions in Modern italy*, Princeton, University Press.

Ralf, Strakloff, (1997), "Participatory Discourses and Practice in a Water Resource Crisis in Sri Lanka" in Sunil, Bastian and Nicola, Bastian, (Ed), (1997), *Assessing Participation: A debate from South Asia* New Delhi, 1997.

Renata, Serra, (2001), Social Capital : Meaningful and Measurable at the State Level, *Economic and Political Weekly*, Vol. XXXVI, Feb. 24, 2001, pp. 693-695.

Rone Loewenson, (2000), "Public Participation in Health" *IDS Bulletin*, Vol. 31, No. 1, January 2000.

Samaranayake, Mallika, (1997), "Significance of Participatory Approaches in Empowering People for Sustainable Development", in Sunil Bastian and Nicola, Bastian, (Ed) (1997) : *Assessing Participation: A debate from SouthAsia* Konark,New Delhi, 1997.

Stirrat, R.L., (1997), "The New Orthodoxy and Truths: Participa-tion, Empowerment and other Buzz Words' in Sunil, Bastian and Nicola, Bastian, (Ed) (1997): *Assessing Participation: A debate from South Asia*, New Delhi.

Sudha, Pai, (2001), "Social Capital, Panchayats and Grass roots Democracy: Politics of Dalit Assertion in Uttarpradesh'. Economic and Political Weekly, Vol. XXXVI, Feb. 24, 2001, pp. 646-654.

United Nations, (1981), Popular Participation as a Strategy for Promoting Country Level action and Natural Development, New York, UNP.

UNCHS, (1984), "Community Participation in the Execution of Low Income Housing Projects" Nairobi, United Nations Center for Human Settlements- HABITAT.

Westergard, K., (1986), "Peoples Participation, Local Government and Rural Development", CDR Research Report. No. 8, Copen Hagen; Centre for Development Research, 1986, p. 25.

Wignaraja, P., (1991), 'Genesis of Intellectual Quest: An Overview', Wignaraja, P., Hussain, A. Sethi, H. Wignaraja, G. (co authors) *Participatory Development : Learning from South Asia.*, Oxford University Press.

3

The Kerala Experiment :

An Overview

Kerala is one of the few States in India, which has honored the constitutional imperative of 1993 landmark legislation, the 73rd and 74th Amendment, and geared all efforts to democratically decentralize the planning mechanism to the grass roots level. Perhaps 'People's Campaign' experimented in Kerala is one of such unique experiments of its kind, in such a scale and magnitude, by any of the Third World Democracies.[1] Inspired by various constitutional and administrative efforts of the Central Government from time to time, also to meet the constitutional obligations, mostly as half hearted attempts, a few State Governments in India like Gujarat, Rajasthan, Karnataka, West Bengal and Maharashtra have attempted to set up decentralized Local Self Government System. All these attempts of decentraliza-tion squarely fit to be categorized as administrative decentralization as none of these States have attempted to implement a truly democratic form of decentralized economic planning by empowering people at the grassroots level, to formulate and implement their own development plans, with the State government remaining as the custodian of funds and playing the role of a facilitator for decentralized planning by providing local level agencies with financial support. (Nair, N.D.G 2000: Palanithurai, K.V 2000). The democratic decentralization experiment in Kerala has been a historical exercise of unique nature, which breaks the traditional methods of decentralization and development planning, viewed from several perspectives. (Franke and Chasin 2000: Chandrasekhar, C.P 2000: Heller 2000: Kunhaman, 2000: Charvak 2000, Sharma, 2003,). This chapter attempts to examine the concrete economic and political environment that served as the background for evolution of the democratic decentrali-zation and participatory planning, the unfolding of unique experiment towards fresh and hither to unknown opportunities for popular participation and empower-ment and the concepts of participation envisaged in the experiment.

THE BACKGROUND

Like any other third world democracy, India is a highly centralized democracy, with strong central government and weak federated State governments. Apart from encroaching to the powers of the federating State governments, central governments were engaged in the control of resources at their disposal and have adopted strategies that result in higher degree of centralization. Decentralisation has remained a long cherished goal of India's economic planning[2] (Nair, N.D.G, 2000). While democratic governance has been confined to central and State levels, bureaucratic administration has been the rule at the lower levels. Hardly, at the levels below State, i.e., District, Municipal or Village, elected bodies existed there to hold the offices. At the power pyramid then existed, the decision has been taken at the central level and development programmes were initiated in the top-to-bottom style. Ordinary citizens did not have any role to play in the design, development and implementation of the plans. The poor, the women and the weaker sections of the population continued to be at the margins, as the mainstream activities were going ahead, bypassing them. Due to a host of reasons, historical, political, and economic, despite the formal consent of all political parties on the need for decentralization, grass roots democracy has remained as a mirage in India (Isaac and Franke, 2000). However, the increased realization and growing conviction that big government cannot achieve growth and development without people's participation and direct initiative have altered the situation in favor of local self-governance.(Singh, Y 2002). The attempts on the parts of the States to decentralize their development programmes have resulted in different models of decentralized planning. All these attempts were partial as well as lacked the real spirit of decentralization and they remained as departmental decentralization than democratic decentralization. (Nair, N.D.G, 2000). A host of reasons was identified as major factors behind the slow progress in true decentralization of economic planning in the country and they focus on the three aspects like 1) Lack of political will, 2) Resistance from higher-level bureaucracy. 3) Absence of a viable institutional setup at the local level.

The trajectory of decentralization in Kerala had been wavering and is a 'story of aborted attempts, unkept promises, and half-hearted efforts' as well as a 'litany of frustrated efforts'. (Raj, 1992 : Gulati 1994: Ramachandran : 1994, Sharma 2003, Isaac 1995). It is also true that Kerala had little experience in democratic decentralization (Nair, N.D.G, 2000). Tracking the history of decentralization in pre-independence Kerala, which had a mixture of direct and indirect colonial rule, is rendered difficult by the fact that the State of Kerala had been under three different administrative regimes. The

Malabar, the Northern part of Kerala, had been under the direct rule of Madras State, ran parallel to that of West Bengal, in the case of decentralization attempts. (Charvak, 2000). The Central and Southern region, constituted by Cochin and Travancore were under the princely rulers until the formation of State in November 1st, 1956, and a uniform system of local body administration become effective in these regions from 1960 onwards, when the Kerala Panchayat Act and Kerala Municipality Act came in to existence. In fact, even before this, attempts for decentralization can be traced in the recommendations of the Administrative Reforms Committee (ARC) in 1957 for the formation of a two-tier set up for local administration with Panchayats and Municipalities at the village level and District Councils at the District level. As Isaac and Franke rightly observed (Isaac and Franke, 2000), the legislations of 1960 and 1961 have ignored the recommendations of ARC in 1957 and appeared as watered down versions. District Development Councils (DDCs) of 1960s, District Planning Offices of 1970s, Preparation of State Component Plans and Tribal Sub Plans at the District level in 1980s and decentralization attempts of the first annual Plan in 1990-91 are the sequential evolution of decentralization efforts in Kerala. All these, though they were in the direction of decentralization, could hardly find any room for people's participation or involvement in the planning process. It was in 1991, after four decades of independence, the district level local bodies in Kerala had the elected representatives. The 73rd and 74th Constitutional Amendments of 1993 had made it imperative on the part of the State Governments to enact laws on local self-government and consequently Kerala Panchayat Raj Bill was introduced in March 1994, which endowed the Grama Panchayats with substantial powers and functions. Besides, the Government of Kerala decided to devolve 35-40 per cent of its Ninth Five Year Plan outlay for development programmes to be formulated and implemented by local self-governments. A mass movement, popularly known as *People's Campaign for Decentralized Planning*[3] was launched to empower local self-governments to prepare plans in a transparent and participatory manner.

The confluence of events that led to the launching of the People's campaign has its roots in the unique socio-economic as well as political environment that has been unfolding in Kerala during the past decades. The development and political imperative of the process of democratic decentralization evolved in Kerala can be understood against the background of distinct socio-economic conditions, political processes, history, topography and cultural context of the State. (Sharma 2003). It is true that Kerala had certain unique advantageous features that often promote such an experiment that involves popular participation in a variety of roles from identification of problems, assessing the resource base, analyzing the options available, understanding the resource constraints and seeking possible alternatives for solving problems and implementing programmes and development projects. (Franke and Chasin 2000, Isaac and Franke, 2000) The achievements in literacy, heightened awareness, sensitivity to public issues, absence of feudal relations that often threatens grass root level democracy, extremely positive attitude conducive for better participation of women etc,. were the positive factors unique to Kerala, which set the ground for such an experiment in Kerala. Apart from these, there are certain other factors, which have played, sometimes as a catalyst and some other times as hindrance, for better participation in democratic decentralization. The affiliation of the majority of the people to political organization, either left or right, as ardent followers or mere sympathizers, had often-complex implication for participatory decentralization. (Muraleedharan, 2001: Sharma 2003). However, the centralized power structure and cadre nature of these organizations have always had a negative implication for true participation. Village communities, being fragmented by social and religious groups with allegiance to political parties have, to a certain extent, barred participation of people. Simultaneously, the employee's organization with centralized structures was hardly operating as support system for democratic decentralization in Kerala. The experience of Total Literacy Campaign (TLC) and the overwhelming presence of numerous voluntary and people's science organizations like Kerala Sasthra Sahithya Parishad (KSSP) were another contributive factor for the successful implementation of the campaign.

Democratic decentralization launched in Kerala has been the political response to Kerala's development crisis and an attempt to get out of the deepening catastrophe to which the State economy has been plunging since the 1970s. (Isaac and Franke 2000). In other words, the People's Campaign for Planning has been the offshoot of the limits of 'Kerala Model' of development, the phenomenon most talked and discussed in international academic circles. A contextual note on this aspect is quite relevant.

THE KERALA MODEL OF DEVELOPMENT

Kerala has offered a unique development experience, sometimes touching the level of a paradox, with a set of well-developed social sectors within a less developed State economy, which became generally acclaimed as 'Kerala Model.'[4] The development experience of Kerala questions the widely held paradigm that first agriculture sector and industrial sector have to develop in order to improve the living standards to the masses. This sequencing of economic growth and mass welfare, which has been sanctified by the experience of developed world, has been questioned by the Kerala experience, which provided the basic requirements of most of her citizens, at a very low level of Per Capita Income and Production, much below the National average. (Issac and Tharakan 1995). The composite index of quality of life has placed Kerala much above the Third World economies. (Zacharia, 1994). The academic reflections on Kerala Model, generally falls in to two variants : First, it was upheld as the ideal and cheap model of development and Second: it is denigrated as a growth-less model, condemning Kerala's achievement as yet another underdevelopment paradigm under colonial and neo-colonial conditions (Mencher 1980: Abdussalam 1994: Umadevi 1994). Isaac and Tharakan (1995) have expressed their reservations on these reflections, underscoring the role played by popular struggles in generating demand for social and welfare measures and making the 'Kerala Model' a reality. Not many regions of the World has been successful in achieving progress in social sectors, as Kerala did, though colonial integration and consequent underdevelopment was a global phenomenon., as they rightly observe. The underlying politics of social improvement and the role the popular struggle plays in molding public demand, which has resulted in social achievements, cannot be ignored, depicting people as passive witnesses or victims of development. There for, even though the basic strategy of effective State intervention was the public provision of education and health with redistribution of assets through land reforms and supportive approach towards better collective bargaining power of the working people, which has contributed towards the model in the making, one cannot overlook the socio, economic and political factors figure in this regard.[5] The high literary tradition of Kerala, reasons for which is quite unexplored, the specific features of pre-colonial agrarian society, active trade links with foreign countries and relations with Buddhist traditions, and the political centralization achieved in the 18th century were some of the factors (Kathleen, 1975: Tharakan 1994). The commercialization of Agriculture accentuated by these factors contributed towards the making of the model to a large extent. (Isaac and Tharakan 1986; Tharakan 1992). Various reform oriented movements like that of Sree Narayana Guru and their impact on various communities like Ezhavas, and the consequent scaling up of preferences for education among the other communities like Nairs, Syrian Christians, and Non-Malayalee Brahmins resulted in viewing education as' a ladder for social and economic upward mobility 'for the lower castes and for 'self-preservation' of the upper castes in the fast changing world. The role of socio-religious movements in generating demand for higher education and consequent improvements in the educational facilities can be vividly understood by comparing the educational system in Malabar region and Southern Region of Kerala. Isaac and Tharakan observed that while under colonial impact the indigenous education system crumbled in Malabar, it got a new lease of life in the South. (Isaac and Tharakan 1995). The torch carried by socio-religious movements was handed over to the communist and socialist movements of 1930s and 1940s, who continued the struggle by organizing people for demands for tenancy rights and land reforms, basic social services and social justice and against discrimination. The Anti-caste campaign and the Punnapra Vayalar Armed Uprising set the background for rapid advancement of left political forces in the 1950s and 1960s. The leftist governments came in to power in Kerala became important nodal points in the process of expansion of the social sectors and welfare measures. (Sunny 1985,1994). Coupled with the provision of health and education facilities, a strong public distribution system, the structural changes like land reforms and the prevailing unique settlement pattern with high density of population resulting in large congregation of villages and towns had contributed towards the efficient distribution of welfare measures. (Cassinander 1994: Sreekumar 1994: Chathopadyaya 1994).

THE CRISIS AND THE DEVELOPMENT IMPERATIVES

The second half of 1970s witnessed the model slipping in to major crisis as creaks began to appear in the economy. The crisis set in motion in the form of severe stagnation in the material production, soaring unemployment, acute fiscal crisis and erosion of sustainability of the social service expenditures, which later became all pervasive. (Kurien. C.T 1994: George, K.K 1994) Production of almost all crops, except that of rubber, declined between 1975-76 and 1986-87. Coconut production fell down in spite of the expansion in the area under cultivation. Decline in Paddy production has made the area dependent on other States for food supplies. Industrial Production has decreased and the share of industrial product in SDP fell sharply. (Subramanian, K.K. 1994). The crisis sneaking in to the traditional sectors had wreck havoc with the employment situation and unemployment got aggravated, open unemployment rate touching three times the national average. (Eapen,1994: Raghavan, P 1994; Mohanan Pillai 1994). The fall in employment and the attitude towards higher education have delivered another paradox that in spite of higher rates of educated unemployment, demand for higher education continued to scale up.

(Isaac and Tharakan 1995). The story of stagnation and crisis in Kerala economy would be incomplete, with out touching the fiscal crisis and foreign remittances to Kerala Economy during this period. Remittances from Middle East, which began to pick up from 1970s, precisely before the appearance of crisis, had contributed more than a quarter of the SDP, at its highest point. The Consumption Per Capita increased, even at the tip of stagnation, trade deficit ballooned, Credit-Deposit Ratio declined to 43 per cent in 1994, while the productive sectors remained stagnant. (Jose Jacob 1994). The fiscal crisis of the State Government took its acute form, revenue account deficit touching 16.5 per cent in 1994-95 from a mere 5 per cent in 1984-85. The failure to generate sufficient budgetary surplus reflected in the low per capita plan outlay of the State, while the State Government has been forced to stick on to the past investment pattern in social sectors due to popular demand. The real social expenditures decreased during 1985-86 and 1991-92 compared to that of 1974-75 and 1984-85 and public distribution system was undermined, posing severe threats to the food security of the State. (Krishnaji 1994). In the International Congress of Kerala Studies, held in 1994, which has discussed the development issues of Kerala in detail, one of the major issues emerged with consensus was the imperative for democratic decentralization and development planning, identifying the startling backwardness in decentralization in the State. (Raphel 1994, Isaac 1995). Consequently, democratic decentralization has been suggested as a remedy to accelerate economic growth and create a new model of growth with equity (Isaac and Franke, 2000). Authors like Oates (1972), Musgrave (1959), Marschak (1959), Ellikson (1991), Wright (1999) Sen (1999) have stood in favor of local-self governance and decentralization as the better option for welfare maximization. Apart from this, democratic decentralization is expected to ensure community participation and grass root involvement in the process of planning and development programmes. As observed by Isaac, the democratic decentralization attempts in Kerala have been to seek the powers of democracy to increase production.

Against this background, Government of Kerala decided to embark on large-scale decentralization of economic planning in 1996. At that time in Kerala, there were 991 Grama Panchayaths, 152 Block Panchayaths, 54 Municipalities, 3 Corporations and 14 District Panchayats. As the first step, government decided to launch the Ninth Five Year Plan of the State as the People's Plan, a democratically decentralized Plan by devolving 35 -40 per cent of the State's annual plan outlay for 1997-98 to three tier Panchayath Raj institutions. The proposal was to launch a *People's Campaign for Planning* in order to ensure maximum participation at the grass root level and to implement the development projects with transparency. This bold decision, historic and path-breaking one, in several contexts, has broken the political and bureaucratic barriers to genuine democratic decentralization of planning with the help of Panchayath Raj Act of 1994. This has replaced the traditional top-to-bottom planning in which (1) there existed no horizontal integration of development plans and programmes prepared, (2) centralized bureaucratic type of planning with out people's involvement and (3) resource limit totally uncared for resulting in several plans and programmes, though vital and significant, left unfinished. Decentralization attempts chalked out in Kerala was an endeavor to do away with all these drawbacks of traditional planning.

PEOPLE'S CAMPAIGN FOR DECENTRALISED PLANNING

Decentralization, as stated earlier, in Kerala has been a unique experiment on several counts. It is a radical experiment in democracy, which has decentralized planning while mobilizing the energy of hundreds of thousands of activists and volunteers to go beyond what government funded projects can accomplish. (Franke and Chasin 2000) Quite contrary to, what is stated in theory, Government of Kerala earmarked 35-40 per cent of the Ninth Five Year Plan fund to the local bodies. In fact, this has reversed the theoretical sequence of decentralization (Isaac and Franke, 2000). Devolution of funds, in large scale, also in the form of grand-in-aids with sufficient autonomy for Local Self Government Institutions (LSGIs) was done without any reservations of the capacity of the newly elected representatives and nascent administration at the LSGIs. Instead of waiting for the LSGIs to gain experience and capacity in handling funds and designing projects for development, they were empowered to implement the projects they have designed with the participation of the people. The democratic decentralization attempts evolved strategies to involve the Grama Sabhas, the people in the planning process and the elected body closest to the people, the LSGIs were the main agencies involved with power to implement the programmes. It encompassed a plethora of strategies like planning, mobilization, building consensus and enhancing capacity, as Sharma puts it. (Sharma 2003.)

Along with the transparency, grass root level participation and involvement of common man, it is the central role assigned to the LSGIs in the preparation and implementation of development projects that constitutes the second unique feature of Kerala's decentralization. The LSGIs were directed to draw a comprehensive plan with need-based and resource based projects. The preparation of projects and plans are to be done in six sequential phases in which participation of people are ensured.

The State Planning Board of Kerala (SPB) views this process of democratization of Kerala as a collective intervention of third world societies for shaping their own destiny, against all odds, defying the logic of market and struggling to change the state policy. (State Planning Board, 1997). The distinguishing features of the process of decentralization in Kerala is that, first it is a people's movement, a movement by people to establish their rightful role in decision making by empowering themselves and the local self governments as opposed to the usual apologetic propaganda to manufacture popular consent for what the State does from above. The People's Campaign was set with the broad objectives of conceptualizing; operationalising and institutionaliz-ing a system of multi-level, people centered planning process appropriate to the regional specificities of Kerala, so that the development crisis of the State can be solved. The campaign also places emphasize on the reconstruction of the current concepts of decentralization and people's planning, enabling State government to translate its commitment to concrete actions by conscientising and mobilizing people in support, harnessing popular opinion and will to overcome resistance offered by vested interests, correcting popular and well trenched but wrong notions of development by initiating development dialogues and introducing plausible alternatives, imparting knowledge and skills needed for local level planning, involving mass organizations and technocrats, and above all evolving and institutionalizing a systematic procedure by which development needs of people are articulated, suitable solutions arrived at, projectised, prioritized, integrated into comprehensive development plans, implemented and monitored with maximum people's participation at all levels. Last, but not least, is the horizontal and vertical integration of planning between various tiers. The campaign was set in motion on 17th August 1996 to be completed in Six sequential phases. A brief note on each phase of the campaign will be contextual.

I PHASE (AUGUST–OCTOBER 1996)

The first phase of the campaign consisted of convening of Grama Sabhas[6] in Village Panchayats and Ward Conventions in Municipalities for identifying local development problems. At this phase, the campaign was oriented towards (i) Ensuring maximum participation of people, particularly, women, the poor, the backward classes and weaker sections of the society, and (ii) Steering the deliberations to identify the needs of the people and finding the gaps in the local development. Around, 650 key resource persons at the State level, 12,000 resource persons at the district level and more than 1,00,000 resource persons at the local level were given training to take an active part in the conduct of Grama Sabhas and group discussions on development sectors, and facilitate structured discussions. (SPB, 1997). Grama Sabha was convened during Sundays and holidays in order to ensure maximum participation. Squads of volunteers visited houses to create awareness about the programme. Colorful posters, advertisements, processions and propaganda using various types of media were resorted. Around 3.5 million persons, roughly 10 per cent of Kerala's population participated in the first Grama Sabha.

II PHASE (OCTOBER –DECEMBER 1996)

The second phase involved the conduct of Local Development Seminars, in which the solutions for the developmental problems identified by the Grama Sabha were attempted. Development reports, the printed document carrying information on sector-wise discussions, socio economic status of the grama panchayats or municipality were prepared based on consolidation of Grama Sabha's reports, review of on going schemes, collection of secondary data, geographical study of the area, and a brief survey of local history. The second phase of the campaign has produced an extensive database on local resources, population and several other variables, a comprehensive survey of all development sectors for all panchayats and municipalities, a list of plausible solutions for the developmental problems and formation of task forces to prepare development projects for each development sector. As reported by State Planning Board, around three lakh people, consisting of representatives from Grama Sabhas, selected representatives, local leaders of political parties, department officials, local experts etc participated in Development Seminars.

III PHASE (DECEMBER 1996-JANUARY 1997)

Sector–wise, task forces constituted at the grass root level, the third phase of the campaign, were to projectise the recommendations and suggestions emerged from the Development Seminars. On the average 12 task forces were constituted in each local body to cover various development sectors. As many as 12, 000 task forces functioned at the grass root level with a total participation of at least 1.2 lakh persons and prepared around one lakh projects for the consideration of the panchayats. The task of preparation of projects were according to the guidelines issued by the State Planning Board and each project prepared has to restrain to the explanation of necessity and relevance of the project, defining the objectives, the process of selection of

beneficiaries, technical analysis and time frame of the works to be completed, agencies and organizations involved in the implementation of the project, investment needed for each activity and identification source of funds, cost-benefit analysis and monitoring activities to be conducted for the maintenance of the project.

IV PHASE (FEBRUARY -APRIL 1997)

The fourth phase involved the task of prioritizing and incorporating of the projects prepared by the task forces into Five-year plans of the panchayats. Each panchayat has to make a clear assessment of their capacity to mobilize the resources from various sources to finance the plan, evolve a development strategy based on problems identified and resource potential of the locality, prioritise and select projects to be implemented and decide on a monitoring mechanism for successful implementation of each project selected. Based on these each panchayat was directed to prepare a plan document, which will elaborately specify the objectives, development strategy, resource mobilization, sectoral programmes, integrated development, welfare of scheduled castes and scheduled tribes, women's development programmes and monitoring.

V PHASE (MARCH 1997- APRIL 1997)

During the Fifth phase of the campaign, the integration of the plans at the Block level and District level is to be completed. These higher-level local bodies have to prepare a comprehensive plan by integrating the schemes and programmes prepared by the local bodies at the panchayats.

VI PHASE (APRIL 1997)

The projects are to be examined from the perspective of technical viability and corrected before they are

implemented. This was assigned to the technical experts who voluntarily took the job. Around 4500 volunteers and 3000 mandatory officials have participated in the programme of technical appraisal of the projects.

PARTICIPATION IN DECENTRALISED PLANNING

These sequential phases of the programme envisage participation of people at grass root level in a variety of forms and roles. Decentralized Participatory Planning in Kerala offers a variety of roles to the common man, as well as women, to participate in the development planning. The participation can be passive, active or decisive depending on the role played by members of grama sabha. He or she can be a simple member participating in the Grama Sabhas and taking part in the deliberations and discussions. A voter can be an active participant by holding some positions like committee members within Grama Sabhas or a decisive participant with some powers to take decisions. Apart from Grama Sabhas or Ward Conventions, Neighborhood Associations, People's Campaign offers several avenues like Development Seminars, Task Forces and Voluntary Labour as the other effective forms of participation.

GRAMA SABHAS

Grama Sabha is the basic institution of decentralized governance. It is the first modern political institution that seeks to place direct political power at the hands of the people, without mediation of elected representatives. (Singh, 2002). As Kothari (1998) has observed, it is the Watchdogs coming between the politician-bureaucratic nexus. Though highly cherished in the Gandhian tradition of decentralization and Gram Swaraj, the concept of Grama Sabha continued to be relegated at various levels of conceptualization and implementation, being trapped in practical impediments and several other bottlenecks, in the history of decentralization. (Isaac and Franke, 2000: Diwarkar 1963: Narayan 1961). The experiments of Grama Sabha produced discouraging results of poor participation also. (Joshy 1995; Patil and Kittur 1990; Bhargava and Raphael 1994 : Raphael 1990). The 73rd and 74th Constitutional Amendment provided the essential constitutional status and protection to Grama Sabha. Along with this, Kerala Panchayat Raj Act of 1994 endowed Grama Sabha with substantial powers and functions. Accordingly, Gram Saba is to be convened at least four times in a year and grama panchayat has to submit the financial account, a detailed statement of works and development activities undertaken. The recommendations of the Grama Sabha are to be given due consideration in all the three tiers of panchayats and the panchayat is accountable to Grama Sabha for the decisions not implemented and answerable to it by stating the reasons for not implementing them. In mobilizing the resources, selection of beneficiaries and mobilizing voluntary labour for the implementation of plans and programmes, Grama Sabha is responsible.

A brief sketch of history of Grama Sabha in India seems to be worthy at this point. It was in 1947 that Grama Sabha appeared in the local government framework for the first time, in Bihar and Rajasthan. However, the pioneering efforts to integrate the Grama Sabha with the Panchayat Raj system materialized in Rajasthan in 1953. Following this, several State Governments attempted to formulate Grama Sabha in their own local bodies, in tune with the thoughts and ideas of Mahatma Gandhi. In the Gandhian philosophy, Gram Swaraj and Grama Sabha are vital elements of democracy playing significant roles in deciding the destiny of the community and people in a region by ensuring the participation of people in the democratic development of the region. Grama Sabha functioning in various States of India are endowed with variety of powers and functions, as seen from the table 3.1.

Grama Sabha is also one of the most important forums where participation of people in development is materialized. The Grama Sabha, since the enactment of 73rd Amendment Act, has become the integral part of the Panchayat Raj System as well as decentralization experiments in Kerala. Grama Sabha have played a very significant part in the decentralization of development planning and participation of people. They are visualized as forums of deliberative direct democracies where people are given a chance for not only electing their representatives, but also for discussing, deciding and participating in the developmental activities of the panchayat. With constitutional provision of mandatory status to Gram Sabha and with the beginning of People's Planning in Kerala, they have come to occupy an important role in the planning process. People are mobilized by local bodies to participate in the Grama Sabha and in order to make it convenient for the people to participate in the Grama Sabha, the meetings were held during holidays. Several types of activities like house-to-house campaigns, processions of cultural troupes and cultural programmes were conducted by the local bodies to mobilise the people to participate in the Grama Sabha. The deliberations were held in small groups of 25 or less, so that the villagers and beginners feel it convenient to participate in the deliberations.

In the villages of Kerala, for the poor and semi-literate house holds with numerous of problems, Grama Sabha has emerged as a forum where they can express their felt needs and problems with legitimate right and power. So far they were totally unheard of such a medium and it offered them a fresh and enlightening experience. This

Table 3.1 : Functions and Duties of Grama Sabha in Various States of India

No	Functions and Responsibilities	States
1.	Auditing of Annual Expenditures	Andhra Pradesh, Bihar, Gujarat, Hariyana, Karnataka, Madhya Pradesh, Punjab, Rajasthan, Sikkim, Andaman and Nicobar, Kerala.
2.	Discussion of the previous years Administration Report	Andhra Pradesh, Bihar, Gujarat, Hariyana, Karnataka, Madhya Pradesh, Rajasthan, Andaman and Nicobar, Kerala.
3.	Direction and Monitoring of Construction Activities	Andhra Pradesh, Bihar, Gujarat, Karnataka, Madhya Pradesh, Punjab, Rajasthan, Sikkim, Andaman and Nicobar, Kerala.
4.	Introduction of New Taxes and Reform of existing Taxes	Andhra Pradesh, Bihar,
5.	Beneficiary Selection	Andhra Pradesh, Assam, Bihar, Gujarat, Karnataka, Kerala, Punjab, Rajasthan, Sikkim, Tamil Nadu, U.P
6.	Voluntary Labour Contribution	Bihar, Gujarat, Karnataka, Kerala, Punjab, Rajasthan, Sikkim, West Bengal, U.P.
7.	Assistance to Developmental Activities	Assam, Bihar, Karnataka, Kerala, Punjab, Rajasthan, Sikkim, U.P.
8.	Undertaking the programmes related to Continuing Education, Family Welfare etc,	Bihar, Karnataka, Kerala, Punjab, Rajasthan, Sikkim, U.P.
9.	Creating a sense of Unity and Community	Bihar, Karnataka, Kerala, Punjab, Rajasthan, Sikkim, U.P, Tamil Nadu, West Bengal.

Contd....

Table 3.1 : (Contd....)

No	Functions and Responsibilities	States
10.	Auditing of Expenditures and getting explanations on the same from the President or Members of Panchayat.	Bihar, Kerala, Punjab, Rajasthan.
11.	Examination of Audit Report	Bihar, Kerala.
12.	Discussion on Budget and Development Programmes	Kerala, Gujarat, Karnataka, Madhya Pradesh.
13.	Evaluation and Monitoring of current development projects	Hariyana, Kerala.
14.	Evaluation of Completed Development Projects	Hariyana, Kerala.

Source : Compiled from N.Jagajivan et.al (ed), Popular Transparency, (Malayalam) Kerala State Planning Board, 2000 .PP 35 -36.

was a clear departure from the traditional planning in which outside experts decided the likely requirements of the people in the villages while plans were prepared and implemented. Grama Sabha also played a very significant role in the creation of awareness among the poor and semi literate people on the decentralization process ongoing in Kerala.

As mentioned earlier, in the first phase of the campaign, in the first Grama Sabha convened, around 3.5 million people participated and the district-wise picture of the participation is given in the Table 3.2 below.

Table 3.2 : District-wise Details of Grama Sabha Participation

District	*Average Attendance by Panchayat*	*Average Attendance by Ward*	*Average as % of Voters*	*Females as % of Voters*	*SC/ST as % of Voters*
Trivandrum	1928	171	11.25	35.01	17.61
Kollam	1810	150	9.37	28.11	13.13
Pathanamthitta	1562	162	12.43	28.9	15.36
Alappuzha	2140	203	14.12	31.49	4.12
Kottayam	1519	143	9.89	26.89	12.38
Idukki	1507	153	12.51	22.45	16.87
Ernakulam	1280	122	8.38	20.26	14.58
Thrissur	1560	142	9.43	27.54	1.48
Palakkad	1477	140	10.44	22.29	4.58
Malappuram	1973	167	12.61	27.43	11.48
Kozhikode	2440	219	15.32	26.76	—
Waynad	2081	185	13.98	22.39	16.15
Kannur	1563	147	11.20	21.94	5.57
Kasargod	1635	150	11.81	20.80	13.11
Total	1737	159	11.38	26.22	8.94

Source : State Planning Board, Thiruvananthapuram, Kerala.

It can be seen that there are inter district variations in participation, and it is highest in Kozhikode and the lowest in Eranakulam District. The average female participation was 26. 22 and on the average11.38 per cent of the voters participated in the first Grama Sabha, implies that on the average 20 to 30 percent of the voters at the rate of one to two persons from each household.

There was also inter-panchayat variation in the participation in Grama Sabha. The table 3.3 given below clearly makes this evident. There were panchayats with participation above 1000 and there were some panchayats where just the minimum required number of participants has attended. One of the important factors that determined the strength of participation in Grama Sabha was the size of wards, the strength of population and density of population. The size of the wards, the strength of population and density of population in the wards has been found to be inversely related to the strength of participation in Grama Sabha. Apart from this urbanization and decrease in the agricultural population

Table 3.3 : Participation in Grama Sabha, Size of Population and Density of Population 1996

No	*Voters in Wards*		*Density of Population*	
	Numbers of Gram Panchyats	*Rate of Partici-pation*	*Numbers of Grama Panchayats*	*Rate of Partici-pation*
Below 1000	50	15.04	490	11.98
1001-1500	537	12.16	250	11.37
1501-2000	354	10.00	126	11.08
2001-2500	32	8.42	58	9.53
25001 & above	6	7.55	53	8.61
Total	979	38	977	38

Source : Statistics related to First grama sabha, 1996-97, People's Campaign Cell, State Planning Board, Thiruvanantha-puram, Kerala.

generally pulled down the strength of participation in Grama Sabha. A more detailed discussion on the determinants of participation is reserved for the subsequent chapters.

The general trend one can observe in the strength of participation in Grama Sabha over time is that, though there has been decrease in participation of people in Gram Sabha, there has been definite variation in the nature and classes of people participated in Grama Sabha. The strength of women and backward classes has been constantly increasing during the three consecutive Grama Sabha since 1996. The table 3.4 provides more details on this aspect. The contextual analysis of this macro picture with the micro picture in the wards of selected Grama Panchayats will be attempted in the subsequent chapters.

Though Grama Sabha has emerged as a livewire in the decentralization structure in Kerala, and the government have geared all its efforts to strengthen its functions and responsibilities through legislations, the severe limitations that one come across in the practical reality seems to be the most haunting issue related to them. From the experiences of social engineers, representatives and trainers associated with the campaign programme, one can find that conduct of Grama Sabha in Kerala are encountering the nascent impediments like, stagnating participation of the people, comparative absence and withdrawal of the middle class and upper class population, absence of creative and vigilant deliberations and discussions and swelling of Grama Sabha with the agenda of beneficiary selection. There are certain Panchayats, who were able to over come this stumbling blocks by alternatively designing their own strategies of enhancing participation by strengthening the Neighborhood Groups (NHGPs here

Table 3.4 : Pattern of Participation in First Three Consecutive Grama Sabha 1996-97

	Average Participation on the basis of								
	Total Voters in the Panchayats No of Grama Sabha			*Total Women in the Panchayat*			*Total Backward Class people in the Panchayat*		
District	*I*	*II*	*III*	*I*	*II*	*III*	*I*	*II*	*III*
Thiruvananthapuram	11.24	9.58	15.75	34.86	41.30	54.28	17.39	19.61	20.37
Kollam	9.37	7.79	10.34	28.31	34.79	45.35	13.13	16.92	17.33
Pathanamthitta	12.62	8.92	14.13	29.12	33.34	43.05	13.29	24.20	23.72
Alappuzha	14.12	12.93	12.93	31.49	39.77	40.90	4.12	15.48	17.39
Kottayam	9.87	8.87	11.90	27.08	34.85	43.77	12.02	14.63	16.74
Idukki	12.51	10.39	11.29	22.45	23.26	29.66	16.87	21.17	26.08
Ernakulam	8.37	8.80	10.12	20.09	27.59	34.00	14.58	15.14	15.42
Thrissur	9.44	8.09	11.65	27.54	33.49	41.20	1.48	20.60	18.44
Palakkad	10.44	10.32	13.04	22.29	28.68	37.00	4.58	23.43	25.85
Malappuram	12.72	10.35	12.78	27.43	28.99	32.14	11.63	14.68	13.90
Kozhikode	15.32	13.59	11.98	26.46	28.60	36.78	11.00	11.95	12.24
Waynad	13.98	10.82	11.45	22.39	25.75	33.73	16.15	17.01	18.02
Kannur	11.20	8.65	7.60	21.94	22.58	33.60	5.57	6.98	7.72
Kasargod	11.81	8.01	10.39	20.80	18.06	28.33	13.11	13.82	16.32
Total	11.40	10.10	11.86	26.19	30.27	38.29	8.82	16.26	17.45

Source : State Planning Board, Thiruvananthapuram, Kerala.

after). One of the serious limitation of Grama Sabha is the size of it. An overwhelming size of 1500 voters cannot be expected to attend the Grama Sabha and participate in the deliberations in an effective way it is expected. In the particular circumstance of Kerala, as some of these Panchayats have successfully experi-mented, it is advisable to organize the NHGPs below the Grama Sabha and delegating some functions to them, leaving the ratification of the decisions at the Grama Sabha later. This experiment has several advantages. This has increased the participation of people in the Grama Sabha and has altered the nature of participation in Grama Sabhas from individual representation to group representations. The NHGPs will enable the effective participation, the meetings are quite informal and the number is much less, and the group leaders will be representing them in the Grama Sabhas later. This, no doubt, is a qualitative improvement in the nature of participation. Above all this has the unique advantage of socializing the individual who is in his march to the position of recluse. The fabric of networking this will weave out can definitely contribute towards a better type of community life in anywhere in the world, in this tuff times of eclipse of such trends. What the Kerala experiment with Grama Sabhas makes it evident is that below the Grama Sabhas, a more comfortable layer of Neighborhood Associations are essential for the effective and transparent system of decentralization.

NEIGHBORHOOD GROUPS

Decentralization procedure in Kerala has paid much attention to make use of the NHGPs even when this micro level organization has not been statutorily and constitutionally protected. In most of the Grama Panchayats in Kerala, NHGPs were regularly summoned for evaluation of performance of local bodies. The local bodies in general were willing to handover some of the functions and responsibilities to the NHGPs. They have successfully contributed towards creating a fabric of positive attitude among the villagers to participatory democracy and people's planning. NHGPs are capable of identifying local development problems; design development projects and implement them with maximum participation. In the selection of beneficiaries, harnessing of popular support and participation for implementation of schemes, mobilizing local work force and material for plan implementation, monitoring and sustaining projects, NHGPs are in a more advantageous position. In reality, the NHGPs have added the dimension of transparency in the exact sense of the term, to the local level planning.

It is the experience with the limitations of Grama Sabhas and the understanding about the untapped infinite potential of Neighborhood Associations as the institutions for grass roots democracy that led to the formation of Neighborhood Associations in several Gram Panahyats in Kerala during the year 1997-98. There are several Grama Panchayats, which has organized Neighborhood Associations even before 1996. The number of Neighborhood Associations in each ward ranged from 10 to 15. The Grama Panchayat has issued clear guidelines regarding the formation of Neighborhood Associations, the structure of them, the membership, the frequency of meetings, meeting places and all. Each Neighborhood Associations will have to cater to around 30 to 35 houses. This varies with every Grama Panchayat depending on the socio economic and topographical environments. A campaign type movement was organized for informing the people about the formation of Neighborhood Associations in each ward. After the first meeting, each Neighborhood Associations has to democratically elect their office bearers. After

the formation of NHGPs, generally, the meeting of the officials and conveners are called and they were given an orientation of the rules and regulations, duties and functions as well as powers of NHGPS. For Ward level activities, Ward level conveners are selected. A Central council of NHGPs for every Grama Panchayat was formed consisting of the Conveners, Elected Representatives, Resource Persons and Grama Panchayat Secretary and President.

NHGPS are empowered to meet at any time for their activities. However, the Central Council of NHGPS have to meet once in a month and whenever the Grama Panchayat Council wants it to meet or for the successful implementation of the Annual Development Projects. The Grama Sabha meetings conducted after the formation of NHGPs granted official recognition to them and then onwards they became one of the critical links in development activities at the local level.

In a democratic type of governance, the real power rests with the people and not with the elected representatives. This has been the basic tenet with which the Neighborhood Groups and their power structure were organized. The absolute power to take any decision rests with the general body consisting of all the members of the Neighborhood Group, while the elected conveners, one of them should be statutorily women, can represent it in the upper level bodies.

The first and foremost function assigned to the NGHPs in most of the Gram Panchyats is the selection of beneficiaries for the development projects implemented by Grama Panchayat. The NHGPs completed this formidable task in a more efficient and transparent way with no complaints arising from the public. Anther task shouldered and effectively completed by the NHGPs was the Comprehensive Family Survey

collecting all kinds of information about the members of family including vital ones like blood group, details of deceases etc. The records prepared by these NHGPs have formed the reliable source of information for planning and implementation of various schemes and projects. Construction of village roads and building and maintenance of drinking water schemes were the two major non-conventional development intervention that the NHGPs under took in some Grama Panchayats. In general, Grama Panchayats were able to utilize the potential of NGHPs in intervening in local development activities and putting them to the most efficient use.

Some of the Grama Panchayats have innovatively harnessed the NHGPs in facilitating meaningful development interventions particularly in the area of employment creation, educational monitoring, cultural integration and development communication; Kumarkam Grama Panchayat of Kottayam District is one among several such Grama Panchayats. Primary education, characterized by a high velocity quality erosion, is the area where the NHGPs in Kumarakam Grama Panchayat have intervened and maneuvered miracles. NHGPs after conducting pre-tests among the primary school children identified the weaker groups and designed supporting packages with the help of unemployed youth and college students of the near by houses. A comprehensive package of support system has been developed with time schedules for home works and physical exercises in daily routines appropriate for each classes and students. The Self Help Groups organized within the network of NHGPs were able to generate employment opportunities and income to the poor women. Another area where the NHGPs have entered is the communication net work organized for providing information on development activities to the public. The NHGP News Paper periodically published by the Grama Panchayat caters to the right of information of the public and provides opportunity for communicating with the public on development issues of the Grama Panchayat.

Kumarakam has illustrated how NHGPs can be instrumental in remolding the community life by fabricating social relations sand witched with mutual concern, affection, care and intimacy, the nostalgic feelings once ruled the life in Kerala's villages. The frequent and periodical meetings of NHGPs provide an opportunity to the village community to see the problems of the neighbors face to face and intervene in them in more positive and creative way for finding solutions from the collective efforts of the community. The author had the first hand experience with the NHGPs in Kumarakam Grama Panchayat of Kottayam District, when the Panchayat Development Committee has conducted a Workshop on NHGPs in 2000. The rays of hope glittering from eyes of poor women who flocked together at the backyards of one of the clay brick houses in Kumarakam Grama Panchayat were eloquent on the dreams blossoming in their minds. Apart from their effective role in meaningful development interventions, NHGPs have proved to be triumphant in weaving the fabric of healthy social and community life, the one that has vanished in the flood of social and economic changes from Kerala's villages. What the development experiences of NHGPs reveal is that there cannot be any ideal and optimal model of NHGPs, but they are unique with the social, economic, political and geographic environments of each Panchayat. It is the local people with their traditional wisdom and current awareness who can decide the structure and functions of the NHGPs in the Panchayats.

DEVELOPMENT SEMINARS

Development Seminars were the second sequential stages of decentralized planning evolved in Kerala in which participation of people is envisioned in a different manner. While Grama Sabhas offered a platform for expressing the felt needs of the people, the development seminars were the avenues for concretizing the local demands, objectively assessing the potential of the locality and availability of resources, integrating the traditional wisdom with modern knowledge and ideas. It is at the development seminars thats the recommendations of the local bodies take the shape of projects. Table 3.5 summarises the details of participation of people in development seminars throughout Kerala. As it can be seen from the table, the average participation for the state as whole is 231.23,

Table 3.5 : Participation of People in Development Seminars

District	*Average No of Participants*
Thiruvananthapuram	234.6
Kollam	291.57
Pathanamthitta	203.00
Alappuzha	253.33
Kottayam	175.89
Idukky	205.29
Ernakulam	196.57
Thrissur	220.75
Palakkad	197.10
Malappuram	273.72
Kozhikode	280.44
Wayanad	235.96
Kannur	250.62
Kasargod	245.56
Total	231.23

Source : Isaac and Franke (2000).

while there are eight districts with above average participation. Participation varied from 175.89 in Kottayam to 291.57 in Kollam.

TASK FORCES

Task forces formed the third phase of the participatory exercise of the people led development in Kerala. With the conclusion of development seminars, the local bodies had a sector wise list of recommendation on what can be done in each ward. Subsequently, they have to carve out detailed projects for the implementation of the schemes finalized in the development seminars. During this more complicated stage, the task force members were to be trained to draft the projects proposals in such a way that individual projects were conceived with awareness of their forward and backward linkages with providing maximum degree of integration.

Task forces offered a unique kind of opportunity for people to participate in a more creative as well as qualitative manner in development planning. Task forces were the key organization of the third phase, in which around a dozen members were included for each sectors and chaired by either a local expert or an elected representative, as preferred by the local body. On the average, each local body had 10 task forces providing the opportunity for more than 100 to participate in it. The district wise picture of participation in task forces is given in the Table 3.6 below. There were nine districts with above average participation in task forces. However, the percentage of female participation is much low and is not more than 20 per cent.

VOLUNTARY LABOUR

Voluntary Labor is another form of participation envisaged in the development paradigm of Kerala's

decentralization programme. The schemes and projects selected were implemented through the beneficiary committees. A portion of the manual labor is to be mobilized through the voluntary labor contributions by the beneficiaries concerned. It has also offered the opportunity for another type of participation and involvement by people in grass root development initiatives.

Table 3.6 : District-wise Profile of Participation in Task Forces

District	*Number of Participants*	*% of Females*
Thiruvananthapuram	114	10.53
Kollam	90	16.67
Pathanamthitta	126	6.35
Alappuzha	110	15.45
Kottayam	69	10.14
Idukky	102	3.61
Ernakulam	120	16.67
Thrissur	211	6.67
Palakkad	114	10.09
Malappuram	109	11.01
Kozhikode	119	11.76
Wayanad	74	18.31
Kannur	95	19.15
Kasargod	59	16.95
Total	1519	11.27

Source : Isaac and Franke (2000).

CONCLUSION

The Campaign for People's Planning in Kerala has been an advancement towards the long cherished goal of participatory democracy. Kerala has witnessed a series of changes in the area of local developmental planning

and participatory democracy since the initiation of the campaign. Development programmes have been made more transparent and popular through the introduction of campaign. By the allocation of 35 to 40 per cent of plan funds to the local bodies government has been, in fact, fulfilling the social and constitutional commitment to the three tier Panchayati Raj System in the country. On the other side, this has provided a golden opportunity to the LSGIs to undertake the historical and constitutional obligation of development intervention by them.

The development programmes designed and implemented by the LSGIs are the illuminating examples of popular participation in design, formulation and implementation and monitoring of the development programmes. The role assigned to the people marks a qualitative improvement indeed in local developmental planning. Development Planning, which has been a official and bureaucratic business, in which local popular participation has been quite unheard of or nominal, has become a campaign in which people participate in from the beginning to end and even after that as monitoring agents for sustaining the projects. Not only there has been change in the role of people, but also there has been the change in the role played by the official machinery in planning. Development planning has been set free from the fruitlessness of routine mechanical exercises and has touched the reality of innovative and creative intervention of all involved in it, particularly the officials and experts. Planning began to call for imaginative and creative involvement on the part of the officials and social engineers. Local resource constraints as well as endowments became one of the prime criteria in decision-making and relevance of the plans and programmes were essentially linked with the local relevance and requirement. Plan monitoring and evaluation, which were confined to futile exercises of accounting and tallying of figures, became meaning full evaluation of costs, benefits and critical analysis of sustainability options with contributions from local community and experts.

The Campaign for People's Planning has altogether altered the perspective of people about local development planning itself. In the bureaucratic top-down planning exercises the objective of participation of people has been the personal gains and benefits associated with it. The major motive behind the individual participation was nothing beyond the personal share of the development benefits and perspective about the social and community goals of development has been practically missing in the perspective about local development planning. Campaign for People's Planning has successfully created such a perspective and it has been novel information that people accepted and internalized. This has awakened the internal wisdom within them and has been operational in ensuring transparency and objectivity in the choice of beneficiaries, projects and plans. The participant observations sessions this author had in the Grama Sabhas and Development Seminars have manifested this live spirit in them. All these have put an end to the filthy stories of corruption, nepotism, criminal waste of resources and misuse of funds associated with bureaucratic planning. The incomplete projects, projects thrown half way and projects became quite irrelevant due to the lag in completion have became the part of history. The system of bureaucratic planning has successfully maneuvered to pull the strings of such a set up by concealing the key pieces of development information from the public. The development information system associated with the Campaign for People's Planning has opened the floodgates of information to the public; this has enabled effective and

meaningful intervention on the part of the people for safeguarding transparency and objectivity in the selection, designing, formulation, implementation, monitoring and evaluation of development projects.

The Campaign for People's Planning has been the confluence of the development trajectory that has been in the making since the formation of the State. The factors that contributed towards the making of the Kerala Model, the forces that led to the plunging of the State Economy in to a deep crisis, the development imperative of a paradigm shift were also analyzed. The development crisis to which the State has been plunging and the development imperative of democratic decentralization has examined in detail in this chapter.

As mentioned earlier, Campaign for People's Planning has successfully created an extremely positive environment for facilitating popular participation in development planning through the construction of grassroots level organizations like Neighborhood Groups, Self Help Groups, Gram Sabha, Ward Conventions and Task Forces. The evolution, the structure, the functions, and contribution of these micro level organizations in the facilitation of participation in local development planning have been explained in detail in this chapter.

NOTES

1. **While portraying these real world experiments as the Empowered Deliberative Democracies, Fung and Wright have cited four of such in the World in which the Kerala and West Bengal Experiments are included among them. See Fung and Wright (2000).**
2. **For a detailed account of Decentralization attempts in India and Kerala see N.D.G.Nair (2000), Isaac and Franke, (2000) Chapter Two.**

3. For a detailed chronicle of Democratic Decentralization in Kerala see Isaac and Franke (2000), Franke and Chasin (2000).
4. Detailed account of various aspects of Kerala Model can be seen in Tharakan 1984, 1998, Kabir and Krishnan 1991, Pillai, P.P 1994, Ramachandran 1996, Franke and Chasin, (2nd Edition) 1996 and several others. For critical comments on the sustainability of Kerala Model see Kannan.K.P (1986, 1999) Subramanian and Mohanan Pillai (1986), Tharaman-galam (1998) Tornquist Olle (1999), UN and CDS (1975), K.T.Ram Mohan (1991, 2000) Franke and Chasin (1991), K.K.George (1993, 1998).
5. An International Congress of Kerala Studies was conducted during August 27-29, 1994, at Thiruvananthapuram, Kerala, India that brought together scholars from different disciplines and concerned socio political activists to discuss various developmental problems of Kerala. The broad perspective emerged in that congress has been examined in Isaac and Tharakan (1995). A historical perspective of making of the Kerala Model has been attempted in this work.
6. Grama Sabhas – Grama Sabhas are the statutory meetings of voters at the wards of Grama Panchayat at the initiative of the Grama Panchayat. All the voters are eligible to be the member of Grama Sabha. On the average, there will be more than 1500 voters in each ward of the Grama Panchayat.
7. Key Resource Persons and District Resource Persons and Resource Persons are voluntary experts who have got training in their tasks associated with Local Level Planning. A detailed account of Resource Persons can be seen in Isaac and Franke (2000).

REFERENCES

Abdussalam , C.A., (1994), "Where does Kerala Stand Among the Indian States in the World ? A Statistical Study Based on Composite Indices of Socio-Economic Development". Paper presented at the Session 7, International Congress on Kerala Studies, August 27-29, 1994, Thiruvananthapuram, Kerala.

Bhargava, B.S. and Raphel, C. Jose, (1994), "Working of Gram Sahbas in Karnataka- A Study at Micro Level" *Journal of Rural Development*, Vol. 13, (2) NIRD.

Chandrasekhar, C.P., (2000), "Democratic Decentralization and the Planning Principle. The Transition from below". Paper Presented at the International Conference on Democratic Decentralisation, May 2000, State Planning Board, Kerala.

Charvak, (2000), "From Decentralization of Planning to People's Planning: Experience of the Indian States of West Bengal and Kerala" Discussion Paper No. 21, Kerala Research Programme on Local Level Developemnt, Center for Development Studies, Thiruvananthapuram, Kerala-695011, Kerala, India. www/http.krpcds.org.

Chattopaddyay, Sreekumar, (1994), "Spatial Settlement System in Kerala" Paper Presented at the Session 20, International Congress on Kerala Studies, August 27-29, 1994, Thiru-vananthapuram, Kerala.

Diwarkar, R., (1963), *Report of the Study Team on Position of Grama Sabha in Panchayati Raj Movement*, Government of India.

Ellickson, Robert, C., (1991), *Order without Law: How Neighbors Settle Disputes*, Harward University Press, Cambridge, Massachusetts.

Franke, Richard W. and Barbara H.Chasin, (1991), "Kerala State, India: Radical Reform as Development". *Monthly Review*, Vol. 42. No. 8, January.

Franke, Richard and Barbara, H. Chasin, (2000), Paper presented at the International Conference on Democratic Decen-tralization.

Fung, Archon and Erik Olin Wright, (2000), "Experiments in Empowered Deliberative Democracy", Paper presented at the Conference on The Real World Utopias Project, January 14-16, University of Wiscosin-Madison.

George, K.K., (1993), *Limits of Kerala Model of Development, Center for Development Studies*, Thiruvananthapuram, Kerala.

——(1998), "Historical Roots of the Kerala Model and Its Present Crisis" *Bulletin of Concerned Asian Scholars*, Vol. 30, No. 4, October-December, pp. 35-40.

——(1994), "Whither Kerala Model" Paper presented at the Session 7, International Congress on Kerala Studies, August 27-29, 1994, Thiruvananthapuram, Kerala.

Gulati, I. S., (1994), "Panchayat Raj and Development" Thomas Nedumkallel Memorial Lecture, Thomas Nedumkallel Memorial Committee, Alappuzha, Kerala.

Isaac, Thomas T.M, Franke, W. Richard, (2000), *Local Democracy and Development: People's Campaign for Decentralised Planning in Kerala,* New Delhi: Left Word.

Isaac, Thomas and Tharakan, Michale, P.K., (1986), "An Enquiry into the Historical Roots of Industrial Backwardness in Kerala : A Study of Travancore Region", Working Paper No. 215, Center For Development Studies, Thiruvanantha-puram.

Isaac, Thomas and Tharakan, Michael, P.K., (1986), "An Enquiry into the Historical Roots of Industrial Backwardness in Kerala: A Study of Travancore Region", Working Paper No. 215, Center For Development Studies, Thiruvanantha-puram.

Isaac, Thomas and Tharakan, Michael, P.K., (1995), "Kerala Towards a New Agenda" *Economic and Political Weekly,* Aug. 5-12, pp. 1993-2004.

Isaac, Thomas, T.M. and Tharakan, Michael P.K., (1986), "Sree Narayana Movement - A Study of Social Bias and Ideological Reproduction" Working Paper, No. 214, CDS, Thiru-vananthapuram, Kerala.

Jose Jacob, (1994), "Role of Financial Institutions in Kerala's Economy" Paper Presented At the Session 20, International Congress on Kerala Studies, August 27-29, 1994, Thiruvananthapuram, Kerala, Abstracts, Vol. 2. pp. 45-46.

Jose, C. Raphel, (1994), "Decentralised Planning in Karnataka" Paper Presented at the Session 22 International Congress on Kerala Studies, August 27-29, 1994, Thiruvanantha-puram, Kerala.

Joshy, G.V., (1995), "Grama Sabhasin Karnataka: A Non Starter" *Kurukshethra, (Sepcial Issue)* Vol. 43 (7), April.

Kathleen, Gough, (1975), "Literacy in Kerala" in Jack Goody, (Ed.) *Literacy in Traditional Societies.* CUP, Cambridge.

Kannan K.P., (1986), "Kerala Economy at the Crossroads ?" *Economic and Political Weekly,* Vol. 25. No. 35-36. September 1-8, pp. 1951-56.

——(1999), "Rural Labour Relations and Development Dilemmas in Kerala: Dilemmas of a Socially Transforming Labour Force in a Slowly Growing Economy" *Journal of Peasant Studies*. Vol. 26. Nos.2 and 3, January/April pp. 140-81.

Kothari, Rajani, (1998), *State Against Democracy: In Search of Human Governance*, Ajantha Publications, New Delhi.

Krishnaji, N., (1994), "Food Security", Paper presented at the Session 20, International Congress on Kerala Studies, August 27-29, 1994, Thiruvananthapuram, Kerala, Abstracts, Vol. 1, pp. 55-56.

Kunhaman, M., (2000), "People's Planning: Planning for a People's Paradigm" Paper presented at the International Conference on Democratic Decentralization, May 2000, State Planning Board, Kerala.

Kurien, C.T., (1994), "Kerala's Development Experience- Some Random Comments about the Past and Some Considerations for the Future".

Marschak, Thomas, (1959), "Centralisation and Decentralisation in Economic Organisation" *Econometrica*, Vol. 27(3), July.

Mencher, Jean, P., (1994), "The Kerala Model of Development: The Excluded Ones" Paper Presented at the Session 7, International Congress on Kerala Studies, August 27-29, 1994, Thiruvananthapuram, Kerala.

Mohanan Pilla, P., (1994), "Small Scale Industries in Kerala : Retrospect and Prospect" International Congress on Kerala Studies, Abstracts, Vol. 2, pp. 65-66, August 27-29, 1994, Thiruvananthapuram, Kerala.

Mridul, Eapen, (1994), "Employment and Unemployment in Kerala: An Analysis of Recent Times" Paper presented at the Session 17, International Congress on Kerala Studies, August 27-29, 1994, Thiruvananthapuram, Kerala.

Muraleedharan, K., (2001), "Women's Participation in Develop-ment and Capacity Building at Grass root Level: Some Observations from Kerala" in S.P.Jain (Eds) *Emerging Institutions for Decentralized Development*. Vol. II, NIRD, Hyderabad.

Musgrave, R.A., (1959), *The theory of Public Finance*, Mac Graw Hill, New York.

Nair, N.D.G., (2000), "People's Planning in Kerala: A Case Study of Two Villages Panchayats". Discussion Paper No. 16. Kerala Research Programme on Local Level Development, Center for Development Studies, Thiruvananthapuram, Kerala-695011, Kerala, India. www/http.krpcds.org

Narayan, J.P., (1961), *Swaraj for the People*, Serve Seva Sangh, Varanasi.

Oates, E.W., (1972), *Fiscal Federalism*, Harcount Brace Jouvanovich, New York.

Palanithurai, K.N., (2000), "Democratic Decentralisation in Tamilnadu: A Status Paper".

Patil, V.T. and Kittur, A.T., (1990), "Grass Roots Democracy: Analysis of Grama Sabhas" *Political Science Review*, Department of Political Science, University of Rajasthan, Jaipur, Jan-Dec.

Raj, K.N., (1992), "Decentralised Development and local Self Government in Kerala" Paper presented at the seminar on Panchayat Raj/Nagar Palika Bill and its Implications for Local Self Governments and Decentralized Development in Kerala" October 2-3, Center for Development Studies, Thiruvananthapuram, Kerala, India.

Raghavan, P., (1994), "Traditional Industries in Kerala: the Need for New Approaches" International Congress on Kerala Studies, Abstracts, August 27-29, 1994, Thiruvananthapuram, Kerala, Vol. 2, pp. 30-31

Ramachandran, (1994), "Kerala in Institute of Social Sciences: 1994, Status of Panchayat Raj in the States of India 1994" Concept, New Delhi.

Raphel, Jos, C., (1990), "Decentralized Planning in Karnataka" (Mimeo), Centre for Development Studies and Activities, Pune.

Rex, A. Cassainder, (1994), "Enigma of Kerala Spatial Formations: Gragara and an Invalidation/Recovery of Desakota Hypothesis" Paper presented at the Session 20, International Congress on Kerala Studies, August 27-29, 1994, Thiruvananthapuram, Kerala.

Sen, Amartya, (1999), *Development as Freedom*, Alfred A. Knopt, New York.

Sharma, Rashmi, (2003), "Kerala's Decentralization; Idea in Practice" *Economic and Political Weekly, Sept. 6, 2003*, pp. 3832-50.

Singh, Yatindra, (2002), "Decentralised Governance in M.P. Experience of the Gram Sabha in Scheduled Areas" *Economic and Political Weekly*, Oct. 5, 4100-4104.

Sreekumar, T.T., (1994), "Understanding Spatial Divide in Kerala" Paper presented at the Session 20, International Congress on Kerala Studies, August 27-29, 1994, Thiruvananthapuram, Kerala.

State Planning Board, (1997), "The People's Campaign for Ninth Plan in Kerala: An Introduction" Government of Kerala, Thiruvananthapuram.

Subramanian K.K. and Mohanan Pillai, P., (1986), "Kerala's Industrial Backwardness:Exploration of Alternative Hypothesis" *Economic and Political Weekly*, Vol. 21. No. 14. April 5, pp. 577-92.

Subramanian, K.K., (1994), "Industrial Strategy for Kerala: A Perspective" International Congress on Kerala Studies, Aug. 27-29, 1994, Thiruvananthapuram, Kerala, Abstracts-A, Vol. II, pp. 19-20.

Tharakan, Michael, P.K., (1994), "Search for Roots of Kerala 'Model' in Colonial and Pre-Colonial History", Paper presented at the Session 42, International Congress on Kerala Studies, August 27-29, 1994, Thiruvananthapuram, Kerala.

Tharakan, Michael, P.K., (1992), "Socio–Religious Reform Movements and Demand for Indicators of Development: Thiruvithamkoor, 1860-1930. in Alok Bhalla and Peer Bumke, *Image of Rural India in the 20th Century*. Sterling Publishers, New Delhi.

Tharamangalam, Joseph, (1998), "The Perils of Social Develop-ment without Economic Growth; the Development Debacle of Kerala, India. *Bulletin of Concerned Asian Scholars*, Vol. 30, No. 1,July- September, pp. 23-33.

Tornquist, Olle, (1999), *Politics and Development: A Critical Introduction*, Sage Publications, London. pp. 145-6.

United Nations (UN) and Center for Development Studies (CDS) (1975) *Poverty Unemployment and Development Policy: A Case Study of Selected Issues with Reference to Kerala*. Department of Economic and Social Affairs, UN, New York.

Umadevi, S., (1994), "Critical Comments on Kerala Model of Development" Paper presented at the Session 7, International Congress on Kerala Studies, August 27-29, 1994, Thiruvananthapuram, Kerala.

Wright, (2000), "Envisioning Real Uttopias" Paper presented at the International Conference on Democratic Decentralisation. State Planning Board, Thiruvananthapuram, Kerala, India.

Zacharia, K.C., (1994), "Demographic Transition in Kerala: A Response to Official Policies and Programmes" Paper presented at the Session 19. International Congress on Kerala Studies, August 27-29, 1994, Thiruvananthapuram, Kerala.

4

Participatory Development in Kerala :

An Assessment

The major questions that puzzle the academicians and policy makers as well are how to mobilize the people to participate in planning and development at grass root levels. The social engineers and resource persons engaged in the mobilization campaigns of Kerala experiment strongly agree with this. Though it is easy to create a tempo of participation by awareness campaigns and processions to awaken the spirit of the people, hardly it needs to be self-sustaining . Sustaining the mood created by the processions and campaign type movements is too difficult and is a complex issue to be addressed. Apart from the macro settings and legal and constitutional environments, there are certain micro and meso level realities that often either hinder or promote participation as the case may be. This chapter has a two fold objective. First, it serves to identify these factors by analyzing the dynamics and the determinants of participation and second, it attempts to draw a picture of the impact of the participatory gender sensitive experiments in Kerala. The study has been conducted based on a sample drawn systematically from Kerala based on relevant parameters like quality and strength of participation in local level planning, as has explained in Chapter Two.

Since this study explores the dynamics and determinants of popular participation in development, the socio economic characteristics of the informants play a crucial role and a detailed profile of the sample area and informants from which the inferences are drawn, will set the appropriate background for a better understanding of the conclusions. Hence, the analysis is to be customarily prefaced by a brief sketch of the sample area and sample of households.

SOCIO-ECONOMIC PROFILE OF THE SAMPLE

The major source of data for the study has been the primary data collected from a sample of two Grama Panchayats of Thrissur District, Kerala viz. Kaiparamba Grama Panchayat of Puzhakkal Development Block and Porkalam Grama Panchayat of Chowannur Development Block. A brief profile of the sample Grama Panchayats will serve towards a far better understanding.

Kaiparamba Grama Panchayat, constituted by Kaiparamaba, Anjoor and Peramanagalam revenue villages has an area of 20.48 square kilometers, a population of 24630 and a density of population of 1133. The Panchayat has a female population of 11924 and a female literacy of 92.64 while the male population is 11286 and male literacy is 90.23 against the total literacy of 95.46. The sex ratio is 1056 and the Panchayat has a work participation rate of 35.46 as a whole, 52.41 for males and 19.31 for the females.

Situated on the sides of Guruvayoor - Kozhikode state highway, Porkalam Grama Panchayat has three revenue villages viz. Akathiyoor, Porkalam and Mangad

under its jurisdiction. With an area of 14.49 square kilometers, the Panchayat houses 14, 244 people of which 7384 are females and 6840 are males. The density of population is 982 and sex ratio is 1080. The Panchayat as a whole has an effective literacy rate of 91.90 in general and 95.03 for males and 89.06 for females. The work participation rate is 33.60 for the general population and 50.86 for male population and 17.61 for females. Table 4. 1 below provides a clear comparative picture of these basic details.

Table 4.1: Socio Economic Profile of the Sample Grama Panchayats

Attributes		*Kaiparamba*	*Porkalam*
Area in Sq.Kms		20.48	14.49
No of Wards		10	8
No of Houses		4439	2580
Males		11286	6840
Females		11924	7384
Total		23210	14224
Density of Population per Sq.Kms		1133	982
Sex Ratio per 1000 males	1056	1080	
Effective Literacy Rate :	General	95.46	91.90
	Male	90.03	95.03
	Female	92.64	89.06
SC Population :	General	2278	2386
	Male	1094	1168
	Female	1184	1218
Work Participation Rate :	General	35.46	33.60
	Male	52.51	50.86
	Female	19.31	17.60

Source : 1. Development Reports and Office records of Grama Panchayats.
2. Panchayat Level Statistics 1995, Department of Economics and Statistics.

The table 4.1 makes it clear that Kaiparamba is a much bigger Grama Panchayat in terms of area, wards, population, number of house holds and density of

population. It has much better work participation rate as well as literacy rate. Kaiparamba Grama Panchayat is divided into 10 wards of which 4 are represented by women and one by backward class member. Similarly, Porkalam Grama Panchayat has eight wards with three women members and one with a member from backward classes. Both these Panchayats have agriculture as the main productive sectors as well as the main source of income to the people. Paddy, Coconut, Arecanut, Pepper, Pineapple, Rubber and Banana are the major crops in Kaiparamba while Paddy, Coconut, Arecanut, Pepper, Banana, Tapioca and Vegetables are in plenty in Porkalam. As given in the Development Report of the Panchayat 1996, only one fourth of the agricultural land has irrigation facility in Kaiparamba and most of the areas suffer from shortage of agricultural laborers, particularly during peak seasons. The higher wage rate in non-agricultural occupations has attracted farm laborers. Increase in the cost of cultivation, lack of proper irrigation facilities, as well as fragmentation of land have made agriculture a least attractive option resulting in leaving around 125 hectares of land uncultivated. As far as Porkalam Grama Panchayat is concerned, as reported by the documents, along with the problems most common in agricultural villages of Kerala, it faces the problems like low productivity as the farmers are sticking on to conventional methods of cultivation.

Both these Grama Panchayats are industrially backward. While Kaiparamba Grama Panchayat has a few Diamond Cutting industries for its credit, Porkalam has some small-scale industries like Plastic, Iron fabrication, Biscuit Manufacturing, Ayurvedic Medicines Production etc. In Kaiparamba, nearly 45 units of the Diamond cutting industry provide employment to 2500 employees, which have relieved the unemployment problem of the youth. It is in a deteriorating condition due to the problems like power crisis, shortage of diamonds and several others and all these have led to the closure of some of them. Around 2500 are unemployed in the Grama Panchayat of which more than 50 percent are women. Among the agricultural laborers, 25 per cent are partially unemployed.

Both of these Grama Panchayats face the acute problems of housing, drinking water and rural transportation. In Kaiparamba, more than 60 per cent of the population has their own facility for drinking water while 10 per cent of them depend on the wells of neighbors. However, more than 25 of the people depend on public water supply schemes in Kaiparamba Grama Panchayat. Hence, most of the area in this gram panchyat faces acute shortage of water during the summer season. The situation in Porkalam Panchayat is not different from this.

PROFILE OF THE SAMPLE OF HOUSEHOLDS

The sample of selected households consists of 511 of which 55 per cent are females and 45 per cent are males. This is the natural outcome of the survey because most of the men at the villages are out of the homes they being the main breadwinners and this pattern have been deliberately left undisturbed as the study had a special emphasise on women and their perspective on participation. More than half of the sample, i.e. 58.50 per cent are non-participants. However, among the group of male informants the share of participants is, as usual, higher than that of the non-participants. The single largest group is the non-participating females constituting 37.76 per cent as given in the Table 4.2.

The Table 4.2 make it clear that participants dominate the sample in the case of males, while the non-participants dominate in the case of females. This is

Table 4.2 : Sex and Category-wise Distribution of Sample Households

Category	*Participant*	*Non-participant*	*Total*
Male	24.08	20.74	44.82
Female	17.42	37.76	55.18
Total	41.50	58.50	100.00

Source : Sample Survey.

more or less a general picture when any aspect of participation in local level planning is considered. It may be interesting and useful to examine the ward wise break up of the sample. Exactly half of the sample is from each Grama Panchayat, though such an equal distribution was not insisted while the distribution between wards is considered. The wards 2 and 8 of the Kaiparamba Grama Panchayat have shared 25.64 per cent and 24.64 per cent each, the wards 2 and 8 of Porkkalam has shared 25.05 per cent and 24.85 per cent respectively. Table 4.3 gives the ward wise details of the sample.

Table 4.3 : Panchayat-wise and Ward-wise Break up of the Sample

Panchayat and Ward	*Participants* *Male*	*Female*	*Total*	*Non-Participants* *Male*	*Female*	*Total*	*Grand Total*
Kaiparamba							
Ward 2(BP)	5.68	2.74	8.42	3.33	13.89	17.22	25.64
Ward 8 (PP)	11.55	7.44	18.98	2.35	3.13	5.48	24.46
Total	17.22	10.18	27.40	5.68	17.03	22.70	50.10
Porkalam							
Ward 2(PP)	3.13	5.09	8.22	6.65	10.18	16.83	25.05
Ward 8(BP)	3.72	2.15	5.87	10.37	8.61	18.98	24.85
Total	6.85	7.24	14.09	17.03	18.79	37.77	49.90
Grand Total	24.07	17.42	41.49	22.70	35.81	58.51	100.00

BP : Better Participation PP: Poor Participation.

Note : In Kaiparamba Panchayat Ward No 2 is the ward with better participation and Ward No.8 is the poor participation ward. But in Porkalam it is the vice versa.

Source : Sample Survey.

OCCUPATIONAL PATTERN OF THE SAMPLE

As usual in any sample survey of the rural Kerala, the unemployed group forming 62.23 per cent dominates the occupational pattern of the sample. The dominance is present in all the groups except that of male participants in which farmers have the majority. (See Table 4.4).

AGE PROFILE OF THE SAMPLE

The average age of the male taken as a group is higher than that of females and sample as whole. Similarly, participating male and participating female have higher average age compared to their counterparts. The age profile given in Table 4. 5 clearly shows that participants generally have a higher age among all groups.

The distribution of sample according to age groups will make the picture clearer. The age group of 26-35 dominates the sample in general, among the females, Non-participants and Male Non-participants. However, among the other groups the age group of 36-45 dominates in the female participants and age group 56 and above dominates among Male Participants. (See Table 4.6).

EDUCATIONAL PROFILE OF THE SAMPLE

The educational profile of the sample given in the Table 4.7 shows that most of the categories is dominated by mere literates. Another point highlighted by the table is that higher qualification and educational levels are followed by a tendency to keep away from the local level planning. Except among the illiterates, among all the other groups, domination is by the non-participating group.

Table 4.4 : Occupational Distributions of the Sample

	Sample					Participant		Non-Participant	
Category	*P*	*NP*	*Total*	*Male*	*Female*	*Male*	*Female*	*Male*	*Female*
Unemployed	18.00	44.23	62.23	16.06	46.17	5.48	12.52	10.57	33.66
Agl. Lab	5.87	2.57	8.44	4.12	4.32	3.32	2.54	0.78	1.70
Farmers	8.02	2.54	10.56	9.39	1.17	6.84	1.17	2.54	00
Business/Self Employed	6.84	8.22	15.06	11.54	3.52	5.67	1.17	5.87	2.35
Service	2.73	0.98	3.71	3.71	0	2.73	00	0.98	00
	41.46	58.54	100.00	44.82	55.18	24.04	17.4	20.74	37.71

Note : P= Participant N=Non Participant.
Source : Sample Survey.

Table 4.5 : Distribution of the Sample According to Age

Category	Average Age
Sample	44.07
Male	48.21
Female	44..07
Participants	47.62
Non-participants	41.55
Male Participants	50.41
Female Participants	43.75
Male Non-participants	45.64
Female Non-participants	39.30

Source : Sample Survey.

Table 4.6 : Age Group–wise Distribution of the Sample-Different Age Groups

Age Groups		Sample				Participants		Non- Participants	
	Sample	Male	Female	P	NP	Male	Female	Male	Female
Below 25	4.7	1.75	7.09	1.89	6.69	1.63	2.25	1.89	9.33
22 – 35	30.72	22.27	37.59	20.28	38.13	16.26	25.84	29.25	43.11
36 – 45	20.94	19.21	22.34	25.00	18.06	20.33	31.46	17.92	18.13
46- 55	19.57	23.14	16.67	21.23	18.39	22.76	19.10	23.58	15.53
Above 55	24.07	33.62	16.31	31.60	18.73	39.02	21.35	27.36	13.99
Total	100	100	100	100	100	100	100	100	100

Note : P=Participant N=Non Participant.
Source : Sample Survey.

Table 4.7 : Distribution of Sample According to Education

Category	*P*	*NP*	*Total*	*P*	*NP*	*Total*	*P*	*NP*	*Total*
Illiterate	3.33	2.15	5.48	0.98	0.20	1.18	2.35	1.96	4.31
Literate	24.07	31.31	55.38	13.50	11.35	24.85	10.57	19.96	30.53
Metric	11.00	16.40	27.40	6.65	6.07	12.72	4.11	10.57	14.68
Degree	2.54	7.24	9.78	2.15	2.35	4.50	0.30	4.89	5.28
P.G	0.59	0.78	1.39	0.59	0.59	1.17	0	0.20	0.20
Others	0.20	0.39	0.59	0.20	0.20	0.40	0	0.20	0.20
	41.73	58.27	100	24.07	20.76	44.80	17.33	37.78	55.20

Note : P= Participant N=Non Participant.

Source : Sample Survey.

RELIGION AND CASTE-WISE BREAK-UP OF THE SAMPLE

The religion and Caste wise break-up of the sample shows that Hindus followed by Christians and Muslims dominate it. While 47.27 per cent of Hindus and 59.68 per cent of the backward castes are participants, Christians and Muslims contributed only around one third of their population as participants. (See Table 4.8)

Table 4.8 : Religion and Caste Wise Distribution of the Sample

Category	*Participants*	*Non-participants*	*Total*
Hindus	30.53	34.05	64.58
	(47.21)	(52.73)	
Christians	8.02	16.83	24.85
	(32.27)	(67.72)	
Muslims	2.94	7.63	10.57
	(27.81)	(72.19)	
Backward Castes	15.07	10.18	25.25
	(59.68)	(40.32)	

Note : Percentages of each component are given below in brackets.

Source : Sample Survey.

PROFILE OF THE FAMILY INCOME OF THE SAMPLE

The average of the family income of the males in the sample is higher than that of both the females and the sample as a whole. Generally, the participating group has a lower average income compared to the non-participating groups. The non-participant groups as a whole has the largest share of 63 per cent of income out of the sample and the participating male has the lowest share of it. i.e. 11.82 per cent as seen from the Table 4.9.

Table 4.9 : Profile of Family Income of the Sample

Category	*Average of Family Income in Rs.*	*Percentage Share of Total Income of the Sample*
Sample	1429.08	
Male	1557.38	48.83
Female	1324.89	51.16
Participants	1267.08	36.78
Non-participants	1543.95	63.21
Male Participants	1481.71	24.95
Female Participants	970.45	23.88
Male Non-participants	1645.19	11.82
Female Non-participants	1488.34	39.33

Source : Sample Survey.

MARITAL STATUS OF THE SAMPLE

Among the sample of informants, 87 per cent are married and the married participants constitute 36 per cent. The non-participant group has 51 per cent as married and 5 percent unmarried. Table 4.10 gives the details of this aspect of the sample.

Table 4.10 : Marital Status of the Sample

%

Category	*Married*	*Unmarried*	*Widows*
Male	36	4	
Female	51	5	4
Total	87	9	4
Male Participants	22	2	0
Female Participants	14	2	2
Participants	36	4	2
Male Non-participants	19	2	
Female Non-participants	32	3	2
Non-participants	47	5	2

The profile given above has drawn a very clear picture of the sample area as well as the sample of households.

It can be seen that both these Grama Panchayats have most of the typical characteristics of any of the present villages of Kerala like dependence on awfully deteriorating agricultural occupations, unemployment, poor housing and drinking water facility, unmatched provisions for education and cultural activities in the village etc. Non-participants dominate the sample in general, but in some rare cases, the domination of participants is seen as in the case of males. When the sample as a whole is taken, it can be seen that it is a true representative of the Kerala state in the case of Participation in local level planning, as the majority of them are non-participants. However, when the males are taken as a group, it can be seen that participants dominate the scene. Ward wise picture of the sample bring out a very clear picture of participation. In the better participation ward, while the female non-participant group dominates, male participants dominate the poor participation ward. However, in the case of Grama Panchayat with poor participation, in both wards it is the non-participant groups that dominate the sample.

The distribution of occupational pattern reveals the fact that unemployed group dominates the whole sample and the non-participants. Most of the agricultural laborers and farmers as well as people from service sector are participants while most of the unemployed kept away from the programme. The participants and male participants have a higher average age compared to that of the sample as well as non-participants. Female participants, Female non-participants and male non-participants have a lower average age.

Age group wise break up of the sample has substantiated this conclusion. The sample as a whole and female has around one third of informants belonging to the age group of 26-35, while the male group has one third of their total belonging to the age group of 56 and above. Among the Participants as a whole and male participants, majority belong to the age group of 56 and above while a major chunk of non-participants and female participants belong to the age group of 26-35. At the same time, both the female and male non-participants have a majority belonging to the age group of 26-35. As the educational profile of the sample reveals, more than 50 per cent of them are mere literate and it is this group, which contributes the largest share to participation. Religion and Caste wise break up of the sample shows that the sample has a majority of Hindus followed by Christian and Muslims. It is to be noted that a substantial contribution of participants has come from the backward classes.

The non-participants have a higher average family income while the participants have lower average family income compared to the average family income of the sample. It can be seen that this trend is common in the case of all groups of participants and non-participants. The sample has more than three fourth of it married and among them more than half are non-participants.

THE BASIC QUESTIONS

The Kerala Experiment in Decentralised Democracy and Participatory Development, in fact, has raised several questions than that it has resolved. Attempts to sort out the basic questions of participation in development is summarized in to the most relevant aspects of participation in development like the dynamics, the determinants, the barriers, the motives and the most crucial one, the impact over the women. This section attempts to explore the questions answered by the Kerala Experiment and the questions raised by it in the context of Participatory Development.

THE DYNAMICS

One of the very serous questions related to participatory development, as mentioned earlier, is how to enhance and sustain effective participation. For obtaining a conclusive answer to this question, one has to address the basic questions like who participates, why they participate and how they participate in development activities. Along with this, the perspective of the non-participating group also has to be analysed to understand why they keep away from this programmes and what can be done to motivate them to participate. From the first set of questions, we get the answers to the questions about the motivations to participation and from the second set of questions, we get some idea about the barriers to participation. The dynamics and process of participation is analysed in terms of the general picture of participation, which comprises the general trends, the spatial variation, and the rural urban dichotomy in participation.

The concept of participation, as far as the campaign for people's planning on going in Kerala, is a comprehensive one. An individual, male or female, can participate in a variety of activities ranging from attending and participating in Grama Sabha meetings, Neighborhood group meetings, Development seminars, Task Forces, Labor mobilisation schemes etc. However, unfortunately, most of the Grama Panchayats are not in the habit of keeping comparable accounts on these various opportunities of participation in their panchayats. Therefore, as far as this study is concerned, for the purpose of analysis, as mentioned earlier, participation is defined as attending the Grama Sabha meetings at their respective wards.

It may be interesting and useful to examine the general trend in participation of people in Grama Sabhas during the three years since 1996. Most of the studies conducted recently (Isaac, Muraleedharan: 2000) have identified positive trends in the strength of participation of the three categories namely Male, Female and Backward classes. Since women's participation cannot be treated in an isolated manner, it is analysed in the general framework of people's participation. The general scenario of participation, particularly that of Women, emerging out of the secondary as well as primary data can be summarised in the following heads.

1. The General Picture
2. The Spatial and Temporal Variation
3. The Rural -Urban Dichotomy

1. The General Picture

It was in the later half of 1996 that the first Grama Sabhas and ward conventions were organized in Kerala. To capture the general picture, the data related to the first Grama Sabhas at the Grama Panchayats and ward conventions at the Municipalities of Thrissur are used. This will help one to assess the efficacy of the campaign and can be useful to work out the dynamics in participation over time during the three years since 1996. The general picture of participation of people in Grama Sabhas and ward conventions is rather promising, but one cannot overlook the distressing elements inherent in it. The participation of Women, i.e. 28.37 per cent, in the first Grama Sabha and ward conventions was encouraging, though it hardly hit the scheduled target of one third. (See Table 4.10 and 4.11) Participation of the other groups, the weaker sections was not much bright, as the figures speak. This indicates that the campaign failed in the initial stages to capture the minds of the target group, particularly, the weaker sections, though it has reached at women to a certain extent.

However, as far as the Municipalities of Thrissur, the urban oriented local bodies, are concerned, the emerging picture seemed to be bright as well as promising. Women's participation has been around 45.76 per cent against the 33.33 per cent target. In the case of weaker sections also, the Municipalities presented a brilliant picture with double that of Grama Panchayats.

Table 4.11: People's Participation in Grama Sabhas and Ward Conventions in Thrissur District in 1996 (Percentages)

Category	*Women*	*Men*	*Backward Class*
Grama Panchayats	28.37	71.63	1.04
Municipalities	45.76	54.01	1.61

Source : Estimated from the Office records of Grama Panchayats and Municipalities in Thrissur District.

Fig 4.1 People's Participation in Grama Sabhas and Ward Conve tions of Thrissur District of Kerala -1996 (%)

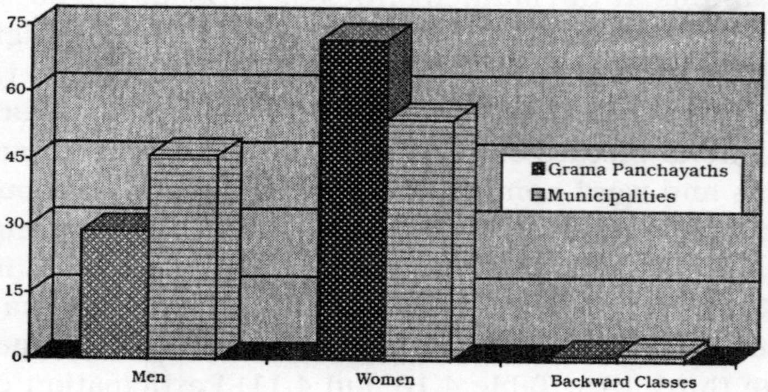

This picture of participation has some message for the planners and policy makers. It is a fact that the Grama Panchayats are mostly in the rural areas and the urban areas have Municipalities instead. In the urban area, the participation of women has exceeded the targets while the rural areas fell short of it by a meager percentage of 1.67. However, the difference between urban and rural participation of women is roughly 17.39 percent. No doubt, this is a sizable variation sufficient to evoke serious concern. Assuming that other things remain the same and the information related to the campaign has been effectively and uniformly communicated in both the urban and rural areas, one can safely infer that the urban settings have some micro level factors that positively influence participation. In other words, urban women in Kerala are in a better position to actively participate in the development activities ,compared to their rural counterparts. A further probe at the household level will reveal the grass root level realities of this dichotomy in rural and urban participation in the case of women.

The general picture of participation of people in Grama Panchayats of Thrissur district and that of sample Grama Panchayats, exhibit different trends when compared. In the case of female participation, the Thrissur District as well as sample panchayats exhibit same trend. In all these cases, there has been a continuous increase in female participation. However, in the case of participation of backward classes, there are uniform trends in Thrissur District and Kaiparamba Panchayat, while a different pattern can be found in the case of Porkalam Grama Panchayat.(See Table 4.12)

2. Spatial and Temporal Variation

Another trend one can observe in the case of Total Participation, particularly in the case of Women, is the

Table 4.12 : Trends in the Strength of Participation in Grama Panchayats of Thrissur District and Sample Grama Panchayats (Percentages)

Category	*1st Grama Sabha*	*2nd Grama Sabha*	*3rd Grama Sabha*	*4th Grama Sabha*	*5th Grama Sabha*
			Kaiparamb Grama Panchayat		
Male	83.76	63.85	64.41	61.32	64.70
Female	16.24	36.15	35.53	38.68	35.30
SC/ST	17.72	16.64	27.39	18.86	26.74
			Porkalam Grama Panchayat		
Male	71.07	62.82	64.69	51.72	49.78
Female	28.92	37.17	35.30	48.27	50.22
SC/ST	23.64	13.13	14.34	9.14	2.98
			Thrissur District		
Male	76.54	72.36	61.57	59.65	59.73
Female	23.40	27.48	38.41	41.28	40.27
SC/ST	6.94	10.55	14.84	16.08	18.67

Source : Office records of Grama Panchayats of Thrissur District.

extreme spatial variation in the strength of participation. It is true that there will not be uniform participation in different Grama Panchayats as they differ in many aspects from the total population to socio, economic, political and other factors like education, occupational structure, income and, of course, political association at various levels. It was found that there is extreme spatial variation in participation of women and other groups across these Grama Panchayats and across the wards internal to the Grama Panchayats. In order to get a clearer idea about variation in participation over time, the co-efficient of variation of strength of participation is worked out for two points of time , i.e. 1996 and 1999 as given in Table 4.13. It can be seen that variation is highest in the case of weaker sections followed by that of women in 1996. In the case of women's participation, it was 59.05 in 1996 and declined to 53.00 in 1999. Coefficient of variation is a ratio of standard deviation and mean multiplied by 100. It is one of the measures of variation in the observations and is positively related to variation. This indicates that spatial variation in the case of strength of women's participation has come down overtime. However, it is in the case of male participation that it has been reduced roughly by half from 45.60 to 28.00, which shows that male participation has become uniform. One can hardly over look the significant reduction in the variation of participation of weaker sections as it has strong message to the policy makers. The variation in the case of weaker sections has been reduced by one fourth indicating a uniform participation on their part throughout the sample area. This strongly communicates the fact that the program has been a tremendous success in generating hope and creating a feeling of relief among the weaker sections who were once kept away from the mainstream of development activities. Thomas Isaac (1997) has rightly observed that these variations cannot be explained in terms of some Socio - Economic and Political factors present in the wards or Grama Panchayats. Still there are some grass root realities unique to each ward or even Grama Panchayats for that matter that crucially determine the strength of participation of women. Some of them are quantifiable, but some escape the attempts of quantification, as they are purely qualitative in nature. To give an example, it may be the local demand for a well, a road, or some other basic facilities that induces the participation of women and weaker sections in one ward or some times a Grama Panchayat. In some other cases, it may be the presence of a charismatic woman leader that motivates them to attend the Grama Sabha. In the course of this study, several women participants were frank to pinpoint the presence of a women leader who inspired them to come over to attend Grama Sabha. In some other cases, there can be an attitudinal factor or the question of awareness on the part of the participants that play a crucial role.

Table 4.13 : Coefficient of Variation of Strength of Participation in Grama Sabhas of Thrissur District in 1996 and 1999

Year	*Women*	*Men*	*Backward Class*	*Total*
September 1996	59.05	45.60	244	44
May 1999	53.00	28.00	68	35

Source : Estimated from the Office records of Grama Panchayats and Municipalities in Thrissur District.

While the analysis of spatial variation looks for the determinants of women's participation, the analysis of dynamics will help to capture the temporal variation of women's participation. In other words, it examines the change in strength of participation over time and tries to sort out the impact of governmental attempts to enhance it during the period of three years over five Grama Sabhas from September 1996 to May 1999. Data related to 10 randomly selected Grama Panchayats in Thrissur District are used for this analysis. A glance at the figures relating to variations in women's participation clearly indicates that there has been a definite upward trend until the fourth Gram Sabha. In the fourth gram sabha, total participation has decreased by 22.70 per cent over the previous one and a major contribution to this decline came from decline in male participation. Actually, there has been only slight decrease in the fourth Grama Sabha in the case of women's participation. Except in this, the up ward trend continues until the fifth one and reaches the peak in the fifth gram sabha. Similar is the trend in the participation of weaker sections. Table 4.14 and Fig 4.14 given below show the temporal trend in the participation of different groups.

Table 4.14 : Temporal Variation in Total Participation in Grama Sabhas from 1996 to 1999 in Thrissur District

(Percentage)

Grama Sabhas Category	*Ist*	*2nd*	*3rd*	*4th*	*5th*
Male	0	1.90	-4.24	-17.97	13.80
Female	0	26.21	57.73	-16.91	21.35
Backward	0	63.83	58.30	-16.24	32.12
Total Participation	0	17.65	9.52	-22.70	12.13

Source : Estimated from the Office records of Grama Panchayats and Municipalities in Thrissur District.

Fig 4.14 Temporal Variation in Participation of Different Groups in Grama Sabhas in Thrissur 1996- 1999

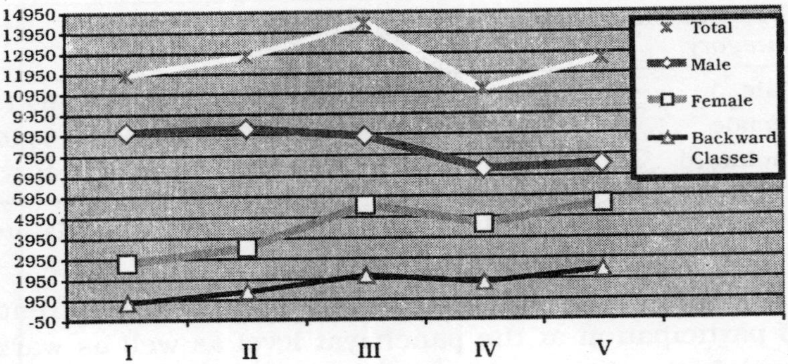

As it is seen from the fig 4.14 there is an upward trend in participation of all groups, until the third Grama Sabha and then the down ward trend begins. As far as the women's participation is concerned, the upward trend continues in the subsequent Grama Sabhas after a slight decline in the fourth Grama Sabhas unlike the Total participation, which declines from the zenith it has reached in the third one. Similar is the trend in the participation of backward classes as it goes up to a higher level after a fall in the fourth one.

A further clear picture can be obtained when the percentage shares of each group are taken and compared. The percentage share of women's participation increases steeply from 23.40 to 44.02 while that of males decreases to 59.13 from a high of 76.54 during the last three years. (See Table 4.15). However, the share of backward classes has been on the upswing from a mere 6.94 per cent to 18.67 registering a more than three fold increase. The fig 4.15 given below graphically illustrates this trend.

Table 4.15 : Percentage Share of Participation of Different Groups in the Grama Sabhas of Thirssur District 1996 - 1999

Grama Sabhas Category	*Ist*	*2nd*	*3rd*	*4th*	*5th*
Male	76.54	72.36	61.57	79.65	59.13
Female	23.40	27.48	38.41	41.28	44.02
Backward	6.94	10.55	14.84	16.08	18.67

Source : Estimated from the Office records of Grama Panchayats and Municipalities in Thrissur.

It is much useful and relevant to examine the trend of participation at the panchayat level as well as ward level. In the subsequent Grama Sabha meetings after the first one held in the middle of 1996, total parti-cipation, male participation and female participation have increased in both the sample panchayats. Female participation has continued the trend until the fifth Grama Sabha in Kaiparamba, where as it has shown a different trend in the Porkalam Grama Panchayat. As the leaders and officials observe that the major determinant of participation in Grama Sabhas is the agenda to be discussed in it. In the meetings in which the beneficiary

Fig 4.15 Trend in Percentage share of Participation of Different Groups in Grama Sabhas of Thrissur Disrtict 1996 - 1999

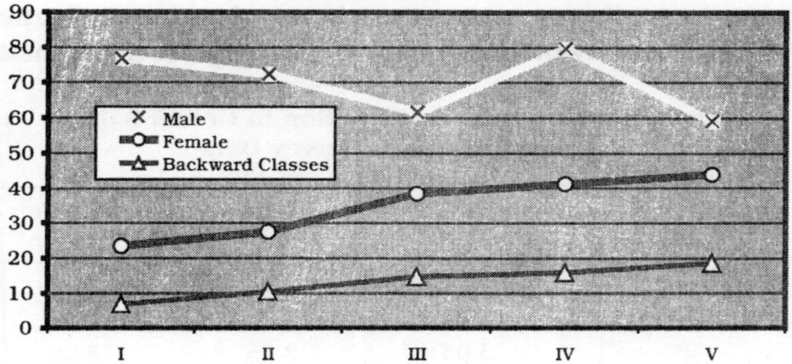

selection is involved, there is much participation. This might have been one of the reasons for increase in participation in certain Grama Sabhas in both Grama Panchayats.

The primary data collected during the survey at the household level gives a different picture about participation. The informants were asked to record the number of Grama Sabha meetings and the Ayalkootam (Neighborhood Association) meetings they have participated and the table 4.16 given below summarises the details. The table shows that more than 60 per cent have participated in more than five Grama Sabhas in the case of sample as a whole and male and female as well. When the data for the Kaiparamba Panchayat is taken separately, it can be seen that more than 70 per cent of the participants have attended five Grama Sabhas. However, for the Porkalam Grama Panchayat, the panchayat with poor participation, the corresponding figures is less than 45 per cent. The inconsistency between the results of primary and secondary data is because primary data is collected from participants alone and they continue to attend the meetings once they become part of the programme. More over there are fresh entrants to this programme when subsequent Grama Sabhas are convened and hence the tempo is sustained.

Table 4.16 : Trends of Participation in Grama Sabhas Based on Sample Survey Data

No of Grama Sabhas	*Total*	*Male*	*Female*
	Sample		
1st	2.36	3.25	1.12
2nd	5.66	3.25	8.99
3rd	10.38	11.38	8.99
4th	11.79	8.94	15.73
5th	69.81	73.17	65.16
	Kaiparamba		
1st	3.33	4.11	2.13
2nd	4.17	2.74	6.38
3rd	9.17	9.59	8.51
4th	10.83	9.59	12.77
5th	72.50	73.97	70.21
	Porkalam		
1st	3.23	3.45	3.03
2nd	11.29	6.90	15.15
3rd	17.74	24.14	12.12
4th	19.35	13.79	24.24
5th	48.39	51.73	45.45

Source : Sample Survey.

3. Rural Urban Dichotomy

As mentioned earlier, one can hardly overlook the striking rural urban disparity in the participation of women, as it has some very serious inferences for the policy makers. This sharp dichotomy in participation extends to other groups also. For analysing this, data related to points of time i.e. September 1996 and May 1999 are collected from 98 gram Panchayats and 7 Municipalities. Women's Participation has been 28.37 per cent in rural area (Gram Panchayats) and 45.76 per cent in urban area (Municipalities) in 1996. It is clear that the share of male participation is less in urban area and high in rural area. Participation of backward classes remained almost the same, though with marginal variations, in both areas in the initial stages of the program. It is when the temporal change in participation of various groups is taken in to account, that the picture gets clearer with the undercurrents being revealed. As it is seen from Table 4.17, during the period between 1996 and 1999, in the urban area, Women's participation has decreased by only 13.95 per cent, while it has a sizable increase of 62.62 per cent in rural areas. In the case of Male participation, the trend has been on the reverse. But in the case of Weaker sections in both areas it has been on the upswing, and that too with a very significant margin of 18 times in rural areas. As far as the total participation is concerned, it has increased in both areas, but the variation was lesser in urban areas with an increase of 1.82 per cent against 9.86 per cent in rural areas.

The analysis of rural urban dichotomy in Women's Participation has some relevant policy implications. There is no doubt that urban settings in Kerala have some positive factors which promotes women's participation in development and it is due to the operation of these factors that the participation of women touched the heights above the scheduled targets. However, the decrease in participation of urban Women by roughly 14 per cent is a matter of serious concern. One can very easily infer that it is not the environment

Table 4.17: Rural and Urban Dichotomy in Participation 1996 -1999 (%)

Particulars	*Female*	*Male*	*Backward Classes*	*Total*
Grama Panchayats				
1996	28.37	71.63	1.04	
1999	41.99	58.01	18.26	
Variation	+62.62	-11.04	18 times	+9.86
Municipalities				
1996	45.76	54.01	1.61	
1999	38.68	64.32	8.85	
Variation	-13.95	+15.59	+82.16	+1.82

Source : Estimated from the Office records of Grama Panchayats and Municipalities in Thrissur District, Kerala.

unique to women that has contributed towards this decline. Simultaneously, male participation has increased by around 16 per cent in urban areas. The participation of Women, men and backward classes has been on the increase and these communicates that the program has generated fresh hopes among them. Governmental efforts to participate more marginalised groups and weaker sections have been a tremendous success in rural areas, whereas it seems that it has suffered a slight set back in the case of urban women, as there has been a retreat of urban women from the arena of development activities.

MOTIVES BEHIND PARTICIPATION

It is one of the very important questions to be asked in relation to participatory approach that why some people participate. Equally important is to look in to question of why some others do not participate. While the answer to the first question is a crucial input for the policy makers to sustain the tempo of participation, the answer to the second question is essential to enhance participation by attracting those who keep away from the programme. In this study, answers to these questions were sought from two sources: the sample survey among the households and focus group discussion with the leaders and resource persons of the programme.

Generally, the social engineers and architects of the campaign in Kerala have been deeply prejudiced to repeatedly state that personal benefits, potential as well as present, are the major motives behind participation. However, the results of the survey present a different picture. It has revealed that along with the personal benefits, equally strong is the thirst for presenting local problems.(See Table 4.18) Social concern reflected in the interest in presenting local problems has emerged as a strong motive for participation, as per the results of sample survey. From the discussions in the Grama Sabhas, it is clear that the male participants and female participants equally share this concern as well. However, among those who participated in the sample survey, the number of males who have expressed this as their chief motive exceeds the females. Similarly, females those who feel that participating in the campaign is important exceeds the males. As mentioned earlier, one will be surprised to see the presence of mothers with feeding babies in the Grama Sabha meetings. All these point out to the deep social consciousness among the female population of Kerala. There are a meager percentage of the participants who follow the dictates of the party men. The details about the beneficiary status of the participants support these arguments. As given in table 4.19 only 40 per cent of the participants are present beneficiaries. Around 45 per cent of the sample are not availing any kind of benefits.

Table 4.18 : Motives Behind Participation-Percentages

Motives	*Total*	*Male*	*Female*
To present the Local Problem	47.64	33.49	14.15
To avail personal benefits	44.33	19.34	24.99
To obey party dictation	2.84	1.42	1.42
Participation very is important	5.19	3.77	1.42

Source : Sample Survey.

Table 4.19 : Beneficiary Status of Participants

Category	*Total*	*Male*	*Female*
Present Beneficiary	40.57	18.86	21.70
Potential Beneficiary	14.15	8.01	6.13
Total	54.72	26.87	27.83

Source : Sample Survey.

THE DETERMINANTS

The most basic question one faces as a facilitator of participation is to how to sustain the tempo of participation once created. To quote the social engineers and officers engaged in the Campaign for People's Planning in Kerala, perhaps, it was the most formidable problems they faced in connection with mobilization of people to the Grama Sabha. In fact, the factors those drive a person to the arena of development activities and factors that deter others from actively participating in development planning and process of development, are to be explored. Apart from the macro settings like the constitutional provisions, institutional settings and organizational atmosphere, there are a host of realities at the grassroots level that hinder and promote participation. This section attempts to examine these determinants of participation.

As a preface, it is necessary to examine the earlier works in this area examining the determinants of

community participation in development. The studies conducted in this area clearly identify a host of factors categorized as Environmental factors affecting participation (Upholf and Cohen 1977: Rao 1982, Smit 1975). The environmental factors suggested by Uphoff and Cohen includes the physical and biological factors like seasonality of production, concentration of settlement patterns, economic factors such as the availability of land and transportation and communication infrastructure; political factors such as the presence of a national ideology supporting democratic procedures: social factors such as social stratification, race and religion, cultural factors such as values discouraging conflict and differential attitudes towards authority, and historical factors such as the nature of previous experience with development efforts. A few programme characteristics like technological level of the activity, resource requirements, flexibility and intensity of staff interaction with the local people were also suggested. The social structure and social positioning of the individual based on the existing social hierarchy will have a deep impact on participation. (Hagen 1962). Kinship and family structures, defining one's access to productive resources, affect the behavior of the people in community participation. (Uphoff and Gillette 1973).

As Giele (1977) argues, family is the major link between the individual and the economy and it distributes authority and privileges between sexes and establishes the relative status of the individuals. The family set up which defines the productive roles of men and women plays a very important role in determining participation. Gender role stereotyping, defined as the extent to which women are restricted to biologically generated but socially determined reproductive-nurturance roles, generally seems to be hampering women's participation (Rao 1982). Women's participation is found to be negatively correlated with the extent of gender stereotyping.

Gillette and Uphoff are of the opinion that there are certain cultural factors such as attitude towards work, leisure and thrift that affect participation, to a certain extent. There are a number of studies that examine the relationship between participation and political factors like political ideology at the national level that promotes democratic procedures of participation in the development process (Huizer 1976: Borda et.al.,1976: Wolf 1977). A few studies identify the organizational factors such as linkages between and among organizations, a multi-sectoral focus and effective leadership affecting the participation in a big way (Uphoff and Esmann 1967:. Choldlin 1967). The participant factors affecting participation have been identified as Consciousness, Self–Confidence, Knowledge, level of organizational and technical expertise, the general level of education and heavy burden of work etc (Hollsteiner 1977: Bosurup 1975 : World Bank 1979).

As mentioned earlier, this study was conducted in the background of Campaign for Peoples' Planning in Kerala. It offers a variety of opportunities for the village people to participate in development from the identification of local development problems to the implementation development programmes and solving it. The capacities with which they can participate also varies from simple observation to active participation in decision-making and implementation of schemes and projects. However, the constraints of data availability often force the study to limit to the Grama Sabha participation alone. Participation in other aspects and stages of local level planning is not officially documented or accounted on a comparative frame in most of these Grama Panchayats. Hence, the participation in this study refers to that in gram shabhas. As far as the general trends in participation is concerned, it was found that it has been varied in different Grama Panchayats and wards, as given by the co efficient of variation for the years 1996 and 1999. It has been the highest in the case of backward classes and lowest in the case of Men in 1966. However, this has reduced much in the case of backward classes and women during the three years ending in 1999. (Muraleedharan.K, 2002) This shows that participation of people, particularly women and backward classes, has been becoming uniform throughout the sample area. Participation of women of the rural oriented local bodies has been on the increase during the three years, while that of the urban oriented local bodies like Municipalities has been decreasing, showing a dichotomy in the participatory behavior of women from urban and rural settings. This has been interpreted in such a way that the women in rural areas were slowly attracted to the campaign and were sticking on to the momentum, while the urban women, better off than the poor rural women, began to keep away from the programme, for reasons unexplored. The social engineers assign this to the attitudinal variations and difference in social and economic background of these two groups.

Assuming a homogenous environment of macro settings like institutional support, organizational insfrastructure, equal opportunities for all with out any artificial barriers, the factors operating at the micro level that promotes or hinders the participation of people in development activities can be categorized as (i) Personal factors and (ii) Social and Economic factors. The personal aspects are those with exclusive personal characteris-tics that vary with individual to individual and places influence on the behavior of the individual in various ways. The personal aspects found to be dominant are the sex, age, marital status, the attitude and motivation. The social and economic factors found to be affecting participation are (i) Income (ii) Education iii) Employment (iv) Political association.

Personal Aspects

It is quite an undisputed fact that sex of the individual constitutes a major determinant of participation and the study has found that majority of the participants are male. In other words, among those participated in the household survey, out of the 55 per cent females and 45 per cent males, 17 percent females and 24 per cent males are participants. Sex continues to be one of the major determinants of participation. This does not imply that there is any kind of discrimination or exclusion of females, as a sizable percentage of female informants are confident enough to deny any male interventions to prevent them from participating in these programmes. In one sense, their male counterparts like husband, father, brother etc represent females in a more harmonious way. Perhaps, it may be household division of labour that has been holding back them. (See Table 4.2).

Age of the informant has appeared to be a very critical factor determining participation. As far as the sample is concerned, the average age of the males is higher than that of the females. Similarly, participants, participating male and participating females as group has a higher average age compared to their counterparts. The general picture emerging is that of youngsters of both sexes keeping away from the programme. Among the females, while the age group of 36-45 dominated the participants, among the males, it is the age of group of above 55 that dominated the sample. (See Table 4.5 and 4.6)

Among the sample of informants, majority of them are married and that marital status of the individual has no particular influence on participation. However, the occupation of the household often plays an important role in determining his behavior in development participation. As far as the sample is concerned, it has shown that majority (62%) of it are unemployed with out any permanent occupations. Quite ironically, this group has contributed the lowest share towards the group of participants. The group of agricultural laborers, farmers and self-employed are the major groups that have contributed more towards participants. (See Table 4.4).

Along with the personal aspects like Education, Age and Occupation, equally strong personal aspect is the motive of the individuals. The motive behind participation can be categorized as (i) Personal benefits, (ii) Interest in Local Development Issues and (iii) External factors such as party directions and dictates. It was found that the social motive like interest in local issues and presenting them in the Grama Sabha are found to be strong among the household informants, compared to the personal motives like availing schemes and projects. More than 52 per cent are participating with this motive.

Social and Economic Aspects

Education as well as income appears to be negatively correlated with the motive for participation. The single major group contributing towards participation, based on education, is the literates. Higher levels of education make negative contribution to participation. It was found that highly educated people participate in local level planning, only when there are positive constraints like deep and effective political association operates to motivate them (See Table 4.7). This should be read together with the doubts of the affluent women during the household discussion sessions that 'what business they have got in local level planning where goats and hens are distributed for poor people'. This clearly shows that education tends to deter participation at the micro level. In this context, it needs to be noted that Isaac and Franke (2000) have found that the regression co-efficient of participation on literacy though positive, is quite negligibly small.

Along with education, the caste hierarchy at high levels often acts as a negative constraint on participation in development. While the backward classes participated actively in the local level planning, the people from forward castes kept away from the programme largely. Another factor, which seemed to influence participation is the income of the family. It was found that family income of the individual seems to be negatively correlated with participation. At higher levels of income, participation tends to be discouraged. The participating group has lower average family income as well as the lower share of total income compared to that of non-participating group in the sample. (See Table 4.9).

Participation is found to be quite an aspect with political dimensions. The political associations of the Grama Panchyat, the president and the ward member often affect participation in some way. Studies in this area have found that political association of Grama Panchayat board has been predominant in deciding the tempo of participation (Muraleedharan. 2001, Isaac and Franke 2002). The conclusions emerging from this study has positively affirmed the conclusions of those conducted at macro level. It was found that political associations ,at any level, to any party, left or right, have been a contributing factor towards enhancing

participation. More than 41.69 per cent of the sample has some association with political parties and out of them, more than half are participants, while the other group, those without any political associations, has contributed less to the group of participants. (See Table 4.20).

Table 4.20 : Political Association of the Informants

Category	*Sample*	*Participants*	*Non-Participants*
With association to Political Parties	41.69	22.90	18.79
With no Association to Political Parties	58.31	18.00	59.10

Source : Sample Survey.

The analysis of determinants of participation in development efforts in the background of campaign for people's planning going on in Kerala since 1996 has shown that in addition to the macro environment like the constitutional, political and institutional factors, there are certain micro level factors that contribute positively or negatively towards participation of people in development. They are categorized as Personal aspects and Social and Economic factors. The Personal aspects included the age, sex, marital status and motives for participation. While the social and economic aspects include income, education, employment, and political association.

THE EXTENT OF PARTICIPATION

The second question crucially related to participation in development is 'how' the people participate. In other words, how far the participant involves in the process of planning and project implementation. With this perspective, participation can be looked from different angles. First, there can be a classification of participation as Passive, Active and Decisive, though the borders often crisscross. Participation is passive when the individuals simply attend the meetings and leave the hall. It becomes active when they assume some role of responsibility like conveners or committees or neighborhood groups. It is decisive when they are assigned with some decision making power. Ultimately, this is a question of 'Voice' and 'Influence'. Those who are able to raise their 'Voice' become active and those who are successful in 'influencing' the outcome of decision-making process become decisive participants. Finally, those fails to either and feels disillusioned becomes the 'exit' and it is at this point that the question of sustaining participation becomes relevant. As far as the sample is concerned, more than 90 per cent of the participants are passive participants and the strength of active participants is less than 8 per cent. Decisive participants forms around 1 per cent among the women as well as in the sample while the male participants even do not have a single decisive participant. (see Table 4.21).

Table 4.21: Quality of Participation (%)

Category	*Male*	*Female*	*Total*
Passive	90	92	92
Active	10	7	7
Decisive	0	1	1
Total	100	100	100

Source : Sample Survey.

Another serious question, often raised in relation to participatory approach by experts and critics, is about the quality of deliberations in the meetings. Therefore, it is necessary to look into the fact that how far these participants take part in deliberations creatively and vigilantly and contribute towards the preparation and implementation of plans and programmes. Whether they are able to present their local problems and get them solved, check the violation of rules and regulations as well as priorities established by norms, by raising their voice are other important issues in this context. The basic preconditions for good quality deliberations are the awareness about the development problems in their area and the ability to present them in the right time, in the right manner and get them solved. As far as the awareness about the local development problems, the male informants (83%) are much better than the female informants (73%) against the general picture of 79 per cent. It can be seen that in good quality deliberations male participants exceed their female counter parts, excepting in getting an assurance that the problem will be looked in to later, as it is evident from the Table 4.22.

Table 4.22 : Quality of Deliberations (%)

Category	*Total*	*Male*	*Female*
Awareness of the local development problems	79	83	73
Successful presentation	73	76	70
Successful in getting them solved	4	5	3
Partly solved	23	25	19
Not attended by the Grama Sabhas	20	23	15
Assurance of Considering later	26	22	37

Source : Sample Survey.

The core objective of Participatory democracy is to ensure that justice is being done to all while plans are prepared and implemented. Each participant in the Grama Sabha needs to be vigilant and closely observing with deep awareness about the proceedings so that no violation of priority is done and all are given their due share in the programmes. They must essentially raise their voice and exert pressure if injustice, nepotism, favoritism or misappropriation is found in the process of plan implementation. Participation is meaningful, significant and efficient as well as effective in all the sense of the term, if and only if, it satisfies the above conditions. In our study, 25 per cent of the participants were vigilant in participation and conscious about the priorities. Male participants (18%) exceed the female participants (5 %) in this aspect also. (See Table 4.22)

Table 4.22 : Vigilance in Participation (%)

Category	*Total*	*Male*	*Female*
Feels that priority has been violated	25	18	7
Raised against this : Always	17	12	5
Raised against this : Sometimes	2	2	0
Raised against this : Never	6	4	2

Source : Sample Survey.

It is clear that those who participate with a sense of justice and sublime motive of the exact sprit of participation is just one fourth of the total and among them those who are willing to raise the voice are much less.

BARRIERS TO PARTICIPATION

As a part of devising the strategy for enhancing participation of people, it requires to get an idea about the perception of non-participants on what really hold back them from participating in the programmes. Revealing their deeply rooted indifference towards the programme, the majority of non-participants, identify lack of free time as the important constraint for participation. More than 52.17 per cent of the non-participants (39.74 per cent of males and 60.26 per cent of females) have stated that they have no sufficient free time to attend the programme. One third of the non-participants felt no interest in the programme and hold that it is not useful to participate, while 5.69 per cent found it inconvenient to participate. (See Table 4.23).

Table 4.23 : Barriers to Participation

Reasons	*Sample*	*Male*	*Female*
No time	52.17	20.74	31.44
No interest	37.79	10.70	27.09
Inconvenient	5.69	3.01	2.68
Not important	2.34	0.33	2.01
No use at all	2.01	0.67	1.34

Source : Sample Survey.

Interest in the programme and permission from the family are another factor, which played an important role in determining participation. Among the female informants of non-participating group, 83.33 per cent are hopeful to obtain permission from their parents, guardians, or husbands whoever it may be, to attend the programme. Same proportion of them, the non-participating informants (of which 32 per cent are females and 20.07 females) have their relatives or other family members as participants of the programme. Inspite of the positive family environment that supports participation, perhaps this might have served as a barrier to participation. Since most of the family, social, communal as well as religious engagements are held during Sundays and holidays which might have a negative impact on participation.

Another crucial factor, which determines the strength of participation is the awareness of the individuals about the local problems. Since the very purpose of the local level planning is to identify the local developmental problem and understand their relevance and significance to the promotion of rural welfare and solving them with local capacity and participation, a minimum level of awareness about the local development issues is the most critical aspect for effective participation. Among the non - participants 53 per cent are not having any idea about the problems at their locality and the possible way of solving it through the local level planning. The lack of awareness about the local problem is acute among the female non-participants. More than two third of them are unaware of the local problem. This agrees with what the women leaders and activists reiterated in the group discussion sessions that awareness creation among the village folk should be given top priority. Besides this, the lack of confidence among them about the potential of local level planning to solve these problems also contributed toward their non-participation. Among the non-participants, 76.92 per cent believed that Grama Sabha could hardly help to solve the problem and improve the situation in the villages. Most of them are unaware about the improvements created by the planning at the local level. While 18.73 per cent believed that there are no development in the panchayat initiated through Grama Sabhas, 49.50 per cent were quite indifferent towards local level planning. One cannot unnotice the fact that the indifference towards local level planning is much wider and deeper among the female non-participants. Apart from this, 67.56 per cent of the non-participants do not feel that it is their duty to attend the Grama Sabhas. Nearly 90 per cent of the non - participants have none of the other female members from their house participating in the Grama Sabha.

The perception of non-participants that emerged from the survey clearly points out to the grim situation of indifference and low awareness among them regarding

the process planning from the grass root level. More than the physical barriers, what strongly deter them from intervening in the planning process are the attitudinal barriers like indifference, lack of awareness, social consciousness and a positive approach towards the new paradigm of development. Those who reflected that they have no sufficient time to share were actually have placed the Grama Sabha meetings and planning process at the lowest of their scale of preference. This implies that they have given it the lowest priority in their daily schedule. Awareness and a strong positive attitude play an important role in this behavior of more than half of the non- participants who have expressed that they have neither time nor interest.

THE IMPACT

The ultimate aim of participation of people, particularly women, is the empowerment of women. Capacity building at the grassroots level is a pre-requisite of empowerment. Though it is a qualitative phenomenon, which hardly compliant to quantified assessment, capacity can be assessed with some criteria. At the local level planning the opportunities for capacity building are immense. The Neighbor hood Groups offers many opportunities to enable the rural women folk to interact in small groups and learn the skills of interaction, good listening and self-expression on the issues of local importance. It was found that participation of women is much higher in neighborhood groups compared to the Grama Sabhas because of the fact that neighborhood groups are very small groups where there is the possibility and ease for much interaction among participating women. Since these are quite informal gathering at the houses of their neighbors and friends, they are supposed to be at home in these gatherings. Self-help groups are another opportunity for the poor

women to be exposed to the fields like banking and credit. This enables them to undertake responsibilities of various kinds at the posts like Secretary, President and Treasurer on a rotation basis. It also offers them exposures to banking activities. Some of the women members were frank enough to reveal that they were scared to drop at a bank premises before they join this kind of groups. They will also learn some motivating techniques while the money lending process starts in their groups. Grama Sabha offers them sufficient opportunities for building capacity for interaction, public speaking and deliberations. Working Committees and Task forces are other openings for capacity building in connection with local level planning. Development Seminars and other specialized conferences offer the women with a lot of exposure to the problems and solutions for their local problems.

Capacity building, because of empowerment exercises in Kerala, is looked from three different angles. In other words, capacity building is assessed using three different criteria like 1). Awareness 2). Interaction and 3). Administration. One cannot deny the fact that these three are the essential qualities of a good leader as well as administrator. Most of the women leaders and women activists and office bearers in the sample area are included in the survey. The temporal change in the capacity of the women leaders in awareness, interaction and administration are assessed during the period of three years from 1995 to 1998.

Awareness : As far as the local level planning is concerned, awareness refers to that about the rules and regulations and local level planning. The women leaders are supposed to be aware about the rules and regulations governing local level planning and various other aspects of planning. It is necessary to look in to the aspect that whether the leaders are able to enrich themselves and enhance their capacity to understand these rules and regulations during the course of their term as leaders and administrators. For this purpose assessing the level of awareness are categorized as very poor, poor, satisfactory, good, and very good. The ranking is done by asking questions related to local level planning and rules and regulations. During the period under study, the percentage of women leaders with low awareness has decreased and high level of awareness has increased. In other words, the capacity to comprehend and understand rules and regulations and other aspects of local level planning on the part of participating women has been increasing during the period under study.

Administrative Capacity : Capacity of administration is another essential capability required for a leader, both women and men. Administrative Capacity, in general, consists of two: capacity to administer the officials and capacity to control the meetings and proceedings. The data related to this aspect reveals that there has been enormous increase in the capacity of women leaders of Kerala during the last three years During the three years the of experience in local level planning there has been tremendous change in the capacity of women leaders in controlling officers and conducting the meetings and proceedings.

Capacity for Interaction : The experience of local level planning has made it clear that there has been tremendous increase in the capacity of women leaders for interaction. No doubt, they cannot function without this capacity. In other words, this is a colossal metamorphosis from timid, shy, introvert, frightened woman folk of the rural villagers of Kerala to bold, motivating, efficient leaders of local level planning. Capacity for interaction is looked from two angles like capacity to interact with people and capacity of public speaking. Capacity of the women leaders to interact with people has increased significantly during the last three years. In 1998, there are not even single women leaders who find it difficult to interact efficiently with public and the percentage of good interactors has increased to 55.38 per cent from 21.37 per cent in 1995. As far as the capacity for public speaking is concerned, nearly half of the leaders are able to address the public meetings satisfactorily, though not much efficiently.

Participation and Capacity building are the integral part of Empowerment. Without either of these, empowerment will remain as quite a distant dream. There fore any discussion on capacity building has essentially to look in to the aspects of participation. Hence, this work has examined the profile of participation as a preface to the analysis of capacity building at grass root level. The strength of participation, spatial variation of participation and the temporal trends in spatial variation are different aspects examined. It was found that the temporal trend of women's participation during the analysis period has been upward and the rate of increase has been significant. The figures of variation in participation overtime has made it clear that participation of women has been simultaneously increasing and becoming uniform throughout the sample area. This is an indication of the success of the programme, which aims at participating one third of women in the campaign.

As far as the determinants of participation are concerned, participation of women in development is a multivariate function of several determinants operating at the grass root level. The political factors have a profound influence on women's participation. Such a statement may take one to a misconception or gross underestimation of the true reality. However, one has to admit that the political association of Grama Panchayat has to do something in mobilizing women to participate in Grama Sabha. It is highly significant to analyze and unearth the grass root level constraints, which either promote or deter women's participation in development. The attempt has been to shed some light to the possible and tentative determinants of Women's participation in development. Apart from the awareness and attitudinal issues of Women that often come in heated debates, some hidden factors determine active participation of Women. Beneath all this superficial factors that motivate and deter, there lies some crucial and grassroots realities that play as undercurrents in taking a women to the arena of development. The urban women who have participated in the campaign do retreat definitely not because of the fact that they are unaware or indifferent. It is at this point that a detailed probe in to the dynamics of grass root realities becomes very significant. What the positive variations in the participation of rural women make out is that once the necessary condition is met, our rural woman will overcome her age-old hurdles to design her fate and advance herself to the mainstream development activities. It is clear that the rural women are in a disadvantaged position when compared to the urban women of Kerala. This disadvantage extends to several aspects of their life like income at her disposal, communication as well as conveyance facilities, attitude of male counterparts, leisure time at her disposal and definitely the family environment. All these factors have a strong sway on her mobility and participation in development. What is more striking is that urban women, with all these advantages and far better environment, is retreating from the arena while the rural women, who are comparatively in disadvantaged position, advance to the mainstream to better their lot. This should be the serious concern of the policy makers.

Capacity building is looked from three different angles i.e., Awareness, Interaction and Administration. Among the women leaders, by the year 1998, there was not all a single women who can be categorized as very poor on the awareness of Rules and Regulations as well as local level planning. Similar is the case of Capacity to conduct meetings and Capacity for interaction. However, their progress in capacity to control officials is not much significant, as there are around 2 per cent of them who can be categorized as poor. Still this achievement is great as it is a journey from poor, timid women to efficient administrators and public speakers of local politics. The social metamorphosis occurred is tremendous and outstanding. This apparently makes clear that the myth of incapable women of our villages can be transformed to the reality of bold, courage and efficient leaders through concerted efforts. The potential remaining untouched is much larger than estimated. Once they were given a chance to participate in these activities, the inertia is broken and it will let loose the unimaginable force required for social transformation.

CONCLUSION

This chapter has attempted to address the basic questions of participation like who participates, why they participate and how they participate in the local level planning in the context of Campaign for People's Planning in Kerala. Along with this, the questions like what is the quality of participation, why do the non-participants keep away from the programme, what are the determinants of participation and what are the barriers to participation were analysed. The impact of empowerment exercises in Kerala also has been examined in detail. It was found that the trends in participation of women and backward classes are common to the sample, district and sample panchayats.

The spatial variation of participation has been analysed and found that participation of the female and the backward classes has become uniform during the last three years. The analysis of temporal variation of participation has illustrated the dynamics of participation. The rural and urban variation in participation of different categories has been analysed.

While analysing the question of why people, particularly women, participate and why do not they participate was analysed and found that the most of the participants are with the motive of presenting their local problems. Family income of the participants, housing conditions of the participants have influenced participation, while access to media has failed in creating any impact. The quality of participation has brought out the fact that most of the participants are passive participants, while small fraction of them is active and decisive. Along with the quality of deliberations, vigilance in participation was also analysed. Most of the non-participants expressed that it is the lack of free time that prevented them from participating in the programmes. Apart from these, the most common reasons of lack of time and interest, they were quite incapable of pointing any serious hurdles in participating in a very serious effort that will have a wide impact on their life and family. This pinpoints to a very sorry state of awareness of on the part of the people regarding the essentiality of participation in programmes like this. More over, they were not sensitized to absorb the fact that planning is their affair and not the affair of the officials and leaders. Still they are under the impression that planning and development is an affair exclusively to be dealt by the government and they have no role to play in it. What is required is the creation of awareness among the people about the relevance of taking part in a programme like this.

The determinants of community participation in development efforts were examined. It was found that apart form the macro environment like the constitutional, political and institutional factors, there are certain micro level factors that contribute positively and negatively towards participation of people in development. They are categorized as Personal Factors, Social and Economic factors and Environmental Factors. The Personal aspects like age, sex, marital status and motives for participation and Social and economic Factors such as income, education, employment, and political association of the individual were found to be influencing participation, while the most significant factors were the environmental factors like awareness and interest. It was found that by creating awareness among the public about the importance of their role in development and providing an extremely positive environment in which the voices of the people are heard and they are able to found a comfortable 'space' for them, community participation can be enhanced.

The analysis of impact has thrown light to the fact that the empowerment exercises in Kerala have been tremendous. The impact has been assessed by examining the capabilities of women leaders and elected representatives during the period before and after the campaign. Capacity building, examined from three angles like Awareness, Interaction and Administration and found that there has been a remarkable change in all these aspects.

REFERENCES

Arunashree, P. Rao, (1982), *Community Participation: Some Issues and Operational Guidelines.* New York: UNICEF.

Boserup, Ester, (1975), *Integration of Women in Development: Why, When, How.* New York: United Nations Development Programme.

Choldin, Harvey, (1967), "Development at Grass Roots". *Community Development Journal*, 6, pp. 39-44.

Fals-Borda, Orlando: Apthorpe, Raymond: and Inayatullah, (1976), "The Crisis of Rural Cooperatives: Problems in Africa, Asia and Latin America" in June Nash, Jorge Dandler.

Nicholas, S. Hopkins (eds.) *Popular Participation in Social Change.* The Hague : Mouton Publishers.

Gillette, Cynthia and Upholf, Norman,T. *Cultural and Social Factors Affecting Small Farmer Participation in Formal Credit Programme,* Ithaca: Cornell University, Center for International Studies, Rural Development Committee.

Giele, Janet, (1977), "Comparative Perspectives on Women" in Giele, Janet and Audrey, C. Smock. (eds.) *Women : Roles and Status in Eight Countries.* New York: John Wiley and Sons.

Hagen, Everette, (1962), "On the Theory of Social Change" Homewood, Illinois : The Dorsey Press, 1962.

Hollnsteiner, Mary Racelis, "People Power: Community Participation in the Planning of Human Settlements" *Assignment Children*, 40, (October/December 1977), pp. 11-47.

Huizer, Gerrit, (1976), "The Strategy of Peasant Mobilisation: Some Cases from Latin America and Southeast Asia" In June Nash, Jorge Dandler, and Nicholas S. Hopkins, (Ed.) *Popular Participation in Social Change.* The Hague: Mouton Publishers, 1976.

Muraleedharan, K., (2002), "Women's Participation and Capacity Building at Grass Root Level: Some observations from Kerala" in S.P. Jain (ed.) *Emerging Institutions for Decentralised Rural Development,* NIRD: Hyderabad.

Smith, M.G., (1975), *Corporations and Society,* Chicago: Aldina publishing Company, pp. 133-163.

Smith, B., (1985), *Decentralisation: The Territorial Dimensions of State.* London: Allen and Unwin.

Uphoff, Norman,T. and Cohen, John, (1977), "Rural Development Participation: Concepts and Measures for Project Design Implementation and Evaluation". Ithaca: Cornel University, 1977.

Wolf, Eric R., (1977), "Kinship, Friendship and Patron-Client Relations in Complex Societies" In Staffen.W.Schmidt, Laura Guasti, Carol.H.Lande and James.C.Scott. (Eds), *Friends,Followers and Factions*. Berkely: University of California Press, 1977.

5

Participatory Development :

Issues and Lessons

Good governance and citizen's participation now form an integral part of development debate. Participation, empowerment and inclusion have become the new development buzzwords. Participatory development, recently, has become an established orthodoxy among development agencies across the political spectrum, from large Western donor agencies to left-of-centered Non Governmental Organizations. Most of the popular intervention methodologies, aimed at stimulating sustainable development, has 'participation' as a major component. It is also being largely realized that Participatory development is the most effective strategy for speeding up economic and social progress in the least developed countries. Community participation has been a key factor in the success of primary health care programs sponsored by nongovernmental organizations in Pakistan. Several South African countries do widely use Participatory development as a strategy for sustainable development. Many organizations and countries at present embrace the philosophy of participatory development in a multitude of ways, either as a means to development or as an end of development itself. Literature on development efforts generated since the last two decades supports this argument in a big way. As a development strategy and as well as tool of intervention, participation is being applied in a variety of areas and fields like Education, Health, Environment protection and sustaining the natural resources. History of traditional communities shows that community intervention for the protection of common properties like watersheds and forests is not a new invention. Now a day, participatory techniques are widely practiced for resource conservation and sustainable development. Apart from this, participatory techniques are being made use of in new areas and regions in a variety of ways. Hence, the lessons and issues from an empirical study are relevant in a multitude of ways. There for an attempt is made here first, to present the contextual issues that crop up when efforts are geared for participatory development and, second, to discuss the critical lessons that learned from such experiments in Kerala and elsewhere.

Gendering governance, earlier, has been understood and interpreted in such a way that it hardly provides any room of political participation of the members of the society in general and women particularly. Accordingly, Politics and Political Participation as such made no appearance in the account of gendering governance. It needs to be redefined and the study of governance must include not only economic management, but also political participation, generally, that in legislative, administrative, institutions, informal groups, movements, and of course institutions of civil society. Viewed from this stance, the Kerala experiment offers the right perspective of gendering governance and empowering women by providing many opportunities for poor women to participate in the political and economic process of planning at the local level from identification of local development problems to the implementation of development projects in various capacities.

What are the contributions of the Kerala Experiment towards Participatory Development and Local Level Planning ? The Campaign for People's Planning in Kerala, as most of its critics may agree, has been an advance towards the long cherished goal of participatory democracy. Kerala has witnessed a series of changes in the area of local developmental planning and participatory democracy since the initiation of the campaign. Development programmes have been made more transparent and popular through the introduction of campaign. By the allocation of 35 to 40 per cent of plan funds to the local body's, the State government has been, in fact, fulfilling the social and constitutional commitment to the three tier Panchayati Raj System in the country. On the other side, this has provided an excellent opportunity to the Local Self Government Institutions (LSGIs) to undertake the historical and constitutional obligation of development intervention by them.

The development programmes designed and implemented by the LSGIs are the illuminating examples of popular participation, particularly female participation, in design, content, formulation, implementation and monitoring of the development programmes. The annual budget of these LSGIs had a Women Component of not less than 10 per cent of the total outlay each year. The role assigned to the people in general and women in particular, marks a qualitative improvement indeed in local developmental planning. Development Planning, which has been an official and bureaucratic business, in which local popular participation has been quite unheard of or nominal, has become a campaign in which people participate from the beginning to end and even after that as monitoring agents for sustaining the projects. Not only there has been change in the role of people, in particular women, but also there has been the change in the role played by the official machinery in planning. Development planning has been set free from the fruitlessness of routine mechanical exercises and has touched the reality of innovative and creative intervention of all involved in it, particularly the officials and experts. Planning began to call for imaginative and creative involvement on the part of the officials and social engineers. Local resource constraints as well as endowments became one of the prime criteria in decision-making and relevance of the plans and programmes were essentially linked with the local relevance and requirement. Plan monitoring and evaluation, which were confined to futile exercises of accounting and tallying of figures, became meaning full evaluation of costs, benefits and critical analysis of sustainability options with contributions from local community and experts.

The Campaign for People's Planning has altogether altered the perspective of people, specifically women, about local development planning itself. In the bureaucratic top-down, planning exercises the objective of participation of people has been the personal gains and benefits associated with it. The major motive behind the individual participation was nothing beyond the personal share of the development benefits and perspective about the social and community goals of development has been practically missing in the perspective about local development planning. Planning and design of development projects from the perspective of women has been totally unheard of so far in the history of development in Kerala. Campaign for People's Planning has successfully created such a perspective and it has been novel information that people accepted and internalized. This has awakened the internal wisdom within them and has been operational in ensuring transparency and objectivity in the choice of beneficiaries, projects and plans. The participant observations sessions this author had in the Grama Sabhas and Development Seminars have manifested this live spirit in them. All these have, to a certain extent, put an end to the filthy stories of corruption, nepotism, criminal waste of resources and misuse of funds associated with bureaucratic planning. The incomplete projects, projects thrown half way and projects became quite irrelevant due to the lag in completion have become the part of history. The system of bureaucratic planning has successfully maneuvered to pull the strings of such a set up by concealing the key pieces of development information from the public. The development information system associated with the Campaign for People's Planning has opened the floodgates of information to the public and this has enabled effective and meaningful intervention on the part of the people for safeguarding transparency and objectivity in the selection, designing, formulation, implementation, monitoring and evaluation of development projects. In fact, contrary to what is held in general regarding the male attitude to female participation, Campaign for People's Planning has successfully created an extremely positive environment for facilitating female participation in development planning through the construction of grassroots level organizations like Neighborhood Groups, Self Help Groups, Gram sabha, Ward Conventions and Task Forces.

What are the issues and lessons that the Kerala Experiment highlights for the concern of the development practitioners and policy makers ?

The first and foremost issue when efforts are geared towards participatory development is that one has to hold a clear perspective about the political, social and cultural context, where the participation is to occur. It is a fact that participation does not take place in vacuum. The development of participation depends on several factors inherent in the context. Perhaps a clear understanding about the political, social and cultural contexts where participation has to occur will make the things easier. With out a clear understanding about the above factors, the chances are more for the failure of efforts for generating sufficient motive and response from the people. There for sufficient time must he provided for analyzing the perspective of stakeholders and identifying the motives and impediments for participation from their view. As a preliminary step, it is better to begin with a stakeholder analysis.

One must note that participatory processes or programmes do not follow a structural, pre-determined and a linear direction. In fact, a spontaneous development gathers momentum from motives and impulses and one cannot set the path earlier. Hence, attempts to implement a participatory development programme based on a pre determined and well-set dimension may hit with failures.

For effective implementation of the participatory development programmes, one should not view participation as merely an input to the implementation of the programme. Participation must be viewed as an underlining operational principle, which should underpin all activities. It is to be regarded as intrinsic to the programmes for development and not simply as an activity that is used from time to time to whip up beneficiary interests. Though several programmes can be cited as the illustrative examples of this, Kerala's campaign for people's planning offers a better example for this perspective. As mentioned elsewhere several times, the campaign for peoples planning in Kerala has the intrinsic strength of being conceived with participation of people as the central theme from the conception to the implementation and monitoring of the development programmes. Participation of people has been viewed as the focal point at all stages of these programme.

What is more important is that one should not confuse between "participation in development" and "participatory development". These concepts are awfully different. Participation in development offers a chance to the people to participate in any type of development activities and probably it may seek to make the more common, top- down and technocratic approach to project development more participatory by evolving some frame works to include the efforts of people in one or the other stage of it. Participatory development implies a radical change in the project management and it is far different from simply adjusting the project planning cycle or allowing for a degree of local involvement. Experience globally supports this argument. There are several examples for failure of development programmes collapsed due to wrong conception of it.

Along with the conceptual clarity essentially required in a participatory form of development, another key element is the training the members of staff receive on the methodologies and techniques and the degree of involvement of the staff in the programme. It is true that the concept of participatory development has revolutionized the project implementation and practice. However, for the operational success, the staff must be trained in participatory development so that they can be effective in promoting and guiding it. This is one of the factors that played behind the success of participatory development in Kerala. The expertise and the voluntary spirit that has been generated out of several popular campaigns like the Total Literacy campaign were the reservoir from which the pool of promoters and volunteers were formed for the campaign for peoples' planning in Kerala.

The most serious issue, according to UN experts on participatory development, is related to the structural relationships and the importance of developing people's capacities and skills to negotiate in a rational manner and seek the resources and changes that improve their lives. This is most important from the point of view of securing a sustainable and long-term development for the people. Unless the capacities of the local people are enhanced, the programme itself loses its sustainability. Literacy, awareness on the local development issues and civic duties, responsibilities and rights are the necessary pre conditions as the background for creating such a capacity. Most of the social engineers and activists of the campaign in Kerala were eloquent on these issues in the focus group discussion sessions.

Apart and along with the macro environment for participation, certain micro level realities also contribute and encourage, some times discourage and deter, participation. They are categorized as Personal Factors, Social and Economic factors and Environmental Factors. The Personal aspects like age, sex, marital status and motives for participation and Social and economic Factors such as income, education, employment, and political association of the individual were found to be influencing participation, while the most significant factors were the environmental factors like awareness and interest. Those who work with participatory development has to clearly identify those micro aspects in advance and design the programme, otherwise the programme will not bring about better results.

Sustaining the tempo of participation is much more difficult than that mobilizing people for the participatory development. The experiment in Kerala had the same problems at different phases. Empty chairs at the Grama sabha venues were often seen at many places. However, thick audience and spontaneous crowds were not uncommon scenes. While designing the schemes for motivating people, it is necessary that they must be capable of sustaining the tempo created in the beginning.

Essentially, a participatory programme will be a success only if it is able to cut the link between personal motives and participation in development. Participation in development motivated by personal motives could not go much far. Sensitizing the people about the essentiality and sustainability of development as well us their role as members of society will perhaps contribute towards better results. At least some of the academicians and experts were prejudiced that most of the female participation is motivated by benefits available to them. The study has shed light to the fact that a sizable share of the sample, particularly women are motivated by local development issues.

Along with enhancing the strength of participation, it is necessary to emphasise on the quality of participation. Participation in the Grama Sabha also serves a vigilant check on the evils of corruption and nepotism. Therefor the participants are to be attuned to raise their voice against all those evils that often ruin the sprit and motive for true participation. As the study pinpoints, such an attempts are hardly traced among the participants, except for a few.

What appears to be more striking from the Kerala experience is the role played by income and education on participation. It was found that at higher levels, both of the variables appear to be deterring participation. The high-income people as well as the highly educated abstained from participating in the programme, for their own reasons. This may be perhaps because the sensitizing efforts were focused on a particular group or the programme has created an impression that participatory development is the business of the poor or the illiterate. This should be seriously viewed and mobilization and awareness creation programmes should be designed so that there is the participation of all groups in the programme.

It is a fact well established from the experiments throughout the globe on participatory exercises that creation of awareness among the participating population is the first and foremost step if any programe of participatory development. The awareness campaigns should be in-built with some simple techniques of motivation for participation in the activities by sensitizing the people on vital issues and problems related to the programme. The Kerala experiment has employed this technique by using small processions and information dissemination systems in order to sensitize and motivate the village folk to participation it the programme.

As far as motivation for participation is concerned, the first and foremost aspect is to create a coducive environment for participation by people. Participation can be fostered only by creating awareness among the public about the importance of their role in development and providing an extremely positive environment in which the voices of the people are heard and they are able to found a comfortable 'space' for them.

Since the beginning, writers like Chambers and Kabeer have been arguing for gendering participation. As it is seen from the assessment of the Kerala scenario, the sex of the participant is a very important explanatory variable in determining participation. As most of the experts argue, despite the aims of participatory development to involve people in development that affects them directly, surprisingly little attention is paid to understand who wants to 'participate', what makes their participation possible, and what is in it for them. Often, participatory processes have left women on the sidelines, along with the gender issues that shape their lives. Combining gender awareness and participatory approaches can be used to unlock men and women's voices for gender redistributive change and gender-sensitive programme and policy development. However, it can be seen that participatory development in the Kerala experience has been perceived with clear gender dimensions of it. The shift of focus from Grama Sabha to the Neighborhood Groups as the operational units of participatory exercises is predominantly with a gender perspective. This attempt was to facilitate the female participant to express their views freely, as it was found that they appear to be more unrestrained in the small groups like Neighborhood groups.

The urgent needs to integrate gender concerns were voiced by several of the experts and writers in this area. One cannot deny the fact that the fields of participatory development and gender studies have remained far apart despite their shared goals like social inclusion and societal transformation. Participatory approaches emerged in an era that centered on male power, perceptions, problems, and experiences. It is also to be noted that the initial emphasis of participatory development was on poverty alleviation. Resistance to what some viewed as a western imposed feminist agenda compounded the approach of participatory development. The strategic gender needs were quite ignored in the initial stages which needs to be again focused in future participatory strategies. The Kerala experiment provides an illustrative example for this approach. The Kerala experiment offers lots of lessons for those who pratice participatory development. The way the mobilization of people was carried out, the motivation techniques, the training for the staff members and resource persons, conduct of Grama Sabhas etc offers a unique pattern that can be replicated elsewhere.

Bibliography

Abdussalam, C.A., (1994), "Where does Kerala Stand among the Indian States in the World ? A Statistical Study Based on Composite Indices of Socio-Economic Development". Paper presented at the Session 7, International Congress on Kerala Studies, August 27-29, 1994, Thiruvananthapuram, Kerala.

Adelman and Morris, (1973), *Economic Growth and Social Equity in Developing Countries.* Stanford: Stanford Univer-sity Press.

Ahmed, I., (1987), "Technology, Production linkages and women's employment in South Asia" *International Labour Review*, 126, pp. 21-40.

Andrea Cornwall, Hentry Lucas and Kath Pasteur, (2000), "Accountability Through Participation: Developing Workable Partnership models in Health Sector"*. IDS Bulletin,* Vol. 31,Number 1, January 2000, Institute of Development Studies, Sussex, pp. 1-14.

Andrea Wilkes, (2000), *The Function of Participation in a Village based health repayment Scheme : What can Participation actually do ? IDS Bulletin,* Vol.31,Number 1, January 2000, Institute of Development Studies, Sussex, pp. 31-36.

Archon Fung and Errik Olin Wright, (2000), *Deepening Democracy: Innovations in Empowered Partcipatory Governance.'* Paper presented at the International Conference on Democratic Decentralisation, May 2000, State Planning Board, Kerala.

Arun Ghosh, (2000), "Globalisation, Decentralisation and Economic Development" Paper presented at the International Conference on Democratic Decentralisation, May 2000, State Planning Board, Thiruvananthapuram, Kerala.

Arunashree, P. Rao., (1982), *Community Participation: Some Issues and Operational Guidelines.* New York: UNICEF.

Aziz, Abdul, (2000), Democratic Decentralisation in Karnataka Paper presented at the International Conference on Democratic Decentralisation, May 2000, State Planning Board, Kerala.

——(1983), *Studies in Block Planning.* Concept, New Delhi.

Baiocchi, Gianpolo, (2000), "Synergising Civil Society. The Politics of Decentralisation in Poto Alegre, Brazil". Paper presented at the International Conference on Democratic Decentralisation, May 2000, State Planning Board, Kerala.

Bandyopadhyay, D., (1997), People's Participation in Planning. Kerala experiment.'*Economic and Political Weekly* Sept.27, pp. 2450-2454.

Bastian, Sunil and Bastian, Nicola, (Ed.) (1997), *Assessing Participation: A debate from South Asia,* New Delhi.

Battivala, S., (1993), "Empowerment of Women in South Asia: Concept and Practices" ASSBAF and FAO, Fredom from Hunger Campaign, Action and Development, 1993.

Bergsten, Fred C., (1993), *The Rationale For a Rosy view'.* The Economist Sept.11, 1993.

Bernstein, H. Campbell, B.,(eds): (1985), *Contradictions of Accu-mulation in Africa.* Bverly Hills, CA : Sage.

Bhargava, B.S. and Raphel, C. Jose, (1994), "Working of Gram Sahbas in Karnataka-A Study at Micro Level" *Journal of Rural Development,* Vol. 13, (2) NIRD.

Bhatnagar, B. and Williams, (1992), (ed.) "*Participatory Development and the World Bank, Potential Directions for Change*", World Bank Discussion Papers. No. 183, October 1992.

Bhattacharya, Dwaipayan, (2001), "Human Development and Civic Community in India : Making Democracy Perform" *Economic and Political Weekly,* Vol. XXXVI, Feb 24, 2001, pp. 673-684.

Biswas, Ajith, (1973), "Central Planning and its Regional Implications with reference to West Bengal" Seminar Paper of Center for Social Science, 24 February 1974, Culcutta, Mimeo.

Black, (1991), *Development in Theory and Practice: Bridging the Gap* Boulder: Westview.

Boserup, Ester, (1975), *Integration of Women in Development: Why, When, How.* New York: United Nations Development Programme.

Boudeville, J.R., (1961), *Regional Economic Planning; Techniques of Analysis,* OECD, Paris.

Brohman, John, (1996), Popular Development : Rethinking the Theory and Practice of Development, Blackwell, Cambridge.

Burkey, S., (1993), *People First, A Guide to Self Reliant Participatory rural development,* London :Zed Books,Landon.

Campbell, T., (1997), Innovation and Risk Taking- The Engine of Reform in Latin American Countries, World Bank.

Chakravarthy, S., (1990), Development Strategies for Growth with equity: The South Asian Experience, Asian Development Review, 8, pp. 133-159.

Chambers, R., (1994), "*Paradigm Shifts and the Practice of Participatory Development", IDS Working Papers No. 2, Institute of Development Studies, Sussex.*

Chambers, R., (1995), "*Paradigm Shifts and the Practice of Participatory Development", Nelson.S and Wright, S. Power and Participatory Development : Theory and Practice.* Intermediate Technology Publications, London.

Chambers, R., (1997), *Where Reality Counts ? Putting the First Last.* International Technology Publications, London.

Chambers, R., (1999), "Preface" (ed.) Shirly.K.While *The Art of Facilitating Participation"* New Delhi: Sage India.

Chandrasekhar, C.P., (2000), "Democratic Decentralization and the Planning Principle. The Transition from below". Paper presented at the International Conference on Democratic Decentralisation, May 2000, State Planning Board, Kerala.

Charvak, (2000), "From Decentralization of Planning to People's Planning: Experience of the Indian States of West Bengal and Kerala" Discussion Paper No. 21, Kerala Research Programme on Local Level Developemnt, Center for Deve-lopment Studies, Thiruvananthapuram, Kerala-695011, Kerala, India.www/http.krpcds.org

Chattopaddyay, Sreekumar, (1994), " Spatial Settlement System in Kerala" Paper presented at the Session 20,

International Congress on Kerala Studies, August 27-29, 1994, Thiru-vananthapuram, Kerala,

Cheema,G. and Rondinelli, (1983), *Decentralisation and Development: Policy Implementation in Developing Countries*, Sage, Landon.

Chenery, H. Ahluvalia, M. Bell,C. Duloy, R., (1974), *Redistribution with Growth*.New York: Oxford University Press.

Choldin, Harvey, (1967), "Development at Grass Roots". *Community Development Journal*, 6, pp. 39-44.

Cohen and Peterson, (1999), *Administrative Decentralisation:* Kumerian Press, West Hartford.

Conyers, D., (1986), Future Directions in Development Studies: the Case of Decentralisation. *World Development*, 1 4 pp. 593-603.

Cook, Bill, (1998), "Participation, Process and Management: Lessons for Development in the History of Organisational Development". *Journal of International Development*, 10 (1) Jan-Feb 1998, pp. 35-54.

Cornie, Jolly, R. and Stewart, F., (1987), *Adjustment with a Human Face: Protecting the Vulnerable Promoting Growth*, Oxford; University Press.

CPGUKAN, (1991), "Community Participation for Health for All" cited in Loenson. R., (1999) *Public Participation in Health Systems in Zimbabwe, Paper for accountability through Participation Workshop*, Brighton Institute of Development Studies.

Crook, Richard, C. and James, C.Mannuel, (1998), *Democracy and Decentralisation in South Asia and West Africa. Participation, Accountability and Performance*. Cambridge, 1998.

Diwarkar, R., (1963), *Report of the Study Team on Position of Grama Sabhasin Panchayati Raj Movement*, Government of India.

Dug Hindson and Bongani Ngqulunga, (2000), "*The Reconstruction of Local Government and the Evolution of Develop-ment Policy in Durban'*. Paper presented at the International Conference on Democratic Decentralisation, May 2000, State Planning Board, Kerala.

Dutta, Choudhari, M., (1989), "New Government Committed to Decentralisation" Economic Times, New Delhi, 13th December.

Ellickson, Robert, C., (1991), *Order without Law: How Neighbors Settle Disputes,* Harward University Press, Cambridge, Massachusetts.

Elson, D., (ed.): (1991), *Male Bias in the Development Process.* New York; Manchester University Press.

Emmerie, J., *(1991), Development Policies and the Crisis of the 1980s.* Paris Development Center for the OECD.

Escobar, A., (1995), *Encountering Development: The making and unmaking of the Third World,* Princeton: Princeton University Press.

Evans, Peter, (1995), *Embedded Autonomy: States and Industrial Transformation*, Princeton University Press, Princeton, NJ.

Evans, Peter, (1997), "Introduction. Development Strategies Across the Public and Private Divide IN Evans, Peter (1997) *State Society Synergy. Governmental and Social Capital,* international and Area Studies, University of California, Berkely.

Fals-Borda, Orlando: Apthorpe, Raymond: and Inayatullah, (1976), "The Crisis of Rural Cooperatives:Problems in Africa, Asia and Latin America" in June Nash, Jorge Dandler.

Fang Jing, (2000), "Participation : A Way to Better Health Outcomes ?" *IDS Bulletine.* Vol 31, No.1, January 2000.

Fenster, T., (1993), "Settlement Planning and Participation Under Principles of Pluralism", *Progress in Planning,* 39, pp.179-242.

Fleming, S., (1991), Between the House Hold: Researching Community Organisations and Networks,*IDS Bulletine,* 22, pp. 37-43.

Francois-Pirre Louis, (2000), "*Decentralisation and Democracy in Haiti*" Paper presented at the International Conference on Democratic Decentralisation, May 2000, State Planning Board, Kerala.

Franke, R.W. Chasin, B.H., (1997), "Power to the Malayalee People" *Economic and Political Weekly* Nov. 29, pp. 3061-3068.

Freire, P., (1996), *Pedagogy of the Oppressed* , Penguin, London.

Fung, Archon and Erik Olin Wright, (2000), "Experiments in Empowered Deliberative Democracy", Paper presented at the Conference on The Real World Utopias Project, January 14-16, University of Wiscosin- Madison.

Gadgil, (1967), *District Development Planning.* Gokhale Institute of Planning and Economics.

Geisler, G., (1993), "Silences Speak Louder than Claims: Gender, Household and Agricultural Development in Southern Africa" *World Development,* 21, 1965-80. p. 2.

George Mathew, (1999), *"People's Plan: Kerala's Success Story", Kurukshethra,* Aug 1999, pp. 15-19.

George, K.K., (1993), *Limits of Kerala Model of Development, Center for Development Studies,* Thiruvananthapuram, Kerala.

——(1998), "Historical Roots of the Kerala Model and Its Present Crisis" *Bulletin of Concerned Asian Scholars,* Vol. 30, No.4, October-December, pp. 35-40.

——(1994), "Whither Kerala Model" Paper presented at the Session 7, International Congress on Kerala Studies, August 27-29, 1994, Thiruvananthapuram, Kerala.

Ghosh, Arun, (1988), "Popular Participation and Decentralised Planning in West Bengal" *Economic and Political Weekly,* 16th January.

Gibson–Graham. J.K., (1995), "Identity and Economic Plurality: Rethinking Capitalism and Capitalist Hegemony" *Environ-ment and Planning. Society and Space,* 13, pp. 275-282.

Giele, Janet, (1977), "Compartive Perspectives on Women" in Giele, Janet and Audrey.C.Smock. (eds.) *Women: Roles and Status in Eight Countries.* New York: John Wiley and Sons.

Gulati, I.S., (1994), "Panchayat Raj and Development" Thomas Nedumkallel Memorial Lecture, Thomas Nedumkallel Memorial Committee, Alappuzha. Kerala.

Gulati, I.S., (1994), *Panchyat Raj and Development,* Msgr. Thomas Nedumkallel Memorial Lecture, Msgr. Thomas

Nedumkallel Memorial Committee, Nirmala College, Muvattupuzha.

Hagen, Everette, (1962), "On the Theory of Social Change" Homewood, Illinois: The Dorsey Press, 1962.

Hahner, J., (1985), "Recent research on Women in Brazil", *Latin American Research Review* 20, pp. 163-79.

Hans Blomkvist and Ashok Swain, (2001), "Investigating Demo-cracy and Social Capital in India". *Economic and Political Weekly*, Vol. XXXVI, Feb 24, 2001, pp. 639-645.

Hirshman, (1982), "The rise and decline of development Econo-mics" in Gersovitz.M, Diaz-Alejandro.C, Ranis, and Rosenwieg, M. (eds) The Theory and Experience of Economic Development: Essays in Honor of Sir.W.Arthur Lewis., Landon, Allen and Unwin 372-90.

Hollnsteiner, Mary Racelis, (1977), "People Power: Community Participation in the Planning of Human Settlements" *Assignment Childern*, 40, (October/December 1977), pp. 11-47.

Honderich, Ted, (1995), "The Question of Well Being and the Principle of Equality" *Mind, Oct.*1981, 90, pp. 481-504.

Huizer, Gerrit, (1976), "The Strategy of Peasant Mobilisation: Some Cases from Latin America and Southeast Asia" In June Nash, Jorge Dandler, and Nicholas S.Hopkins, (Ed.) *Popular Participation in Social Change*. The Hague: Mouton Publishers, 1976.

Huq, Mahabub Ul, (1976), *The Poverty Curtain: Choice for the Third World* , New York, Columbia University Press.

Hyden, (1997), "Civil Society, Social Capital and Development: Dissection of a Complex Discourse, Studies in Comparative International Development, 32,I, pp. 3-30.

Isaac, Thomas and Tharakan, Michale, P.K., (1986), "An Enquiry into the Historical Roots of Industrial Backwardness in Kerala: A Study of Travancore Region", Working Paper No. 215, Center For Development Studies, Thiruvanantha-puram.

Isaac, Thomas, T.M. and Michael Tharakan, P.K., (1995), "Kerala: Towards a New Agenda" *Economic and Political Weekly* Aug 5-12, pp. 1993-2004.

Isaac, Thomas.T.M., (1997), "People's Plan Campaign; An interrim Assessment and Response to a Critique" in Chekkutty, N.P., (ed).

Isaac, Thomas, T.M., (1999), "The Socio Economic Political Context of Decentralised Planning Campaign" Paper presen-ted at the National Workshop on Decentralised Gover-nance, KILA, Thrissur.

Isaac, Thomas, T.M, Harilal, K.N., (1997), 'Planning for Empower-ment : People's Planning for Decentralised Planning in Kerala'. *Economic and Political Weekly* Jan 4-11, pp. 53-58.

Isaac, Thomas, T.M, Franke, W.Richard, (2000), *Local Democracy and Development: People's Campaign for Decentralised Planning in Kerala,* New Delhi: Left Word.

Jain, L.C., et.al (1985), *Grass with out Roots,* Sage, New Delhi.

Jenny Litrack and Seddon Jessica, (1999), "Decentralisation: Briefing Notes" World Bank Institute Working Papers. p. 3.

Jha, S.N., *Introduction, in* Jha.S.N., and Mathur, P.C., (1997), (Ed.) *Decentralisation and Local Politics: Readings in Indian Government and Politics" Sage, New-Delhi.1997.*

John, Brohman, (1996), *Popular Development. Rethinking the Theory and Practice of Development* Cambridge, Black-well.

John Harris, (2000), *The Dialectics of Decentralisation: Comparing National Experiences.* Paper presented at the International Conference on Democratic Decentralisation, May 2000, State Planning Board, Kerala.

John Kurian, (1997), "On Development and Public Action: A Reflection on the Kerala Experience" in Sunil, Bastian and Nicola, Bastian, (Ed) (1997): *Assessing Participation: A debate from South Asia* Konark, New Delhi, 1997.

John T. Milimo, (2000), "Health Partnership in Zimbabwe", *IDS Bulletin,* Vol 31, Number 1, January 2000, Institute of Development Studies, Sussex, pp. 43-48.

Jose, C. Raphel, (1994), "Decentralised Planning in Karnataka" Paper presented at the Session 22 International Congress on Kerala Studies, August 27-29, 1994, Thiruvanantha-puram, Kerala.

Joshy, G.V., (1995), "Grama Sabhasin Karnataka: A Non Starter" *Kurukshethra, (Sepcial Issue)* Vol. 43 (7), April.

Kambou, S.D., (1999), "How do we define participation? Are we ready to embrace it?" In: Embracing participation in development: worldwide experience from CARE's Reproductive Health Programs with a step-by-step field guide to participatory tools and techniques. Wisdom from the field, edited by Meera Kaul Shah, Sarah Degnan Kambou, Barbara Monahan. Atlanta, Georgia, CARE, Health and Population Unit, 1999 Oct. :1.1-1.10.

Kannan.K.P., (1986), "Kerala Economy at the Crossroads ?" *Economic and Political Weekly,* Vol. 25, No. 35-36. September 1-8, pp. 1951-56.

——(1999), "Rural Labour Relations and Development Dilemmas in Kerala: Dilemmas of a Socially Transforming Labour Force in a Slowly Growing Economy" *Journal of Peasant Studies.* Vol. 26, Nos. 2 and 3, January/April, pp. 140-81.

Karl, Marilee, (1995), *Women and Empowerment: Participation and Decision Making.* Zed Books, Landon.

Kathleen, Gough, (1975), "Literacy in Kerala" in Jack Goody, (Ed.) *Literacy in Traditional Societies.* CUP, Cambridge.

Kaufman, Michael and Alfonso, Hafoldo Dilla, (1994), *Community Power and Grassroots Democracy: Transformation of Life.* Landon: Zed Books.

Keller, B. and Mbewe, D., (1991), Policy and Planning for the Empowerment of Zambia's Women Farmers, *Canadian Journal of Development Studies,* 12, pp. 75-88

Khan, A., (1987), "A Comment on Professor Chakravarty's Paper" in Toye, J. (ed) *Development Policies and the Crisis of the 1980s* Paris : Development Centre for the OECD, pp. 96-100.

Kirsten, Westergard, (1986), "Peoples Participation, Local Government and Rural Development", CDR Research Report. No. 8, Copen Hagen; Centre for Development Research, 1986, p. 25.

Kitching, (1982), *Development and Underdevelopment in Historical Perspective: Populism, Nationalism and Industrialism,* New York: Methuen.

Kohen, M. and K. Deutsch, (1980), "Decentralisation and Development: Policy Implementation in Developing Countries, Landon: Sage.

Kothari, Rajani, (1998), *State Against Democracy: In Search of Human Governance*, Ajantha Publications, New Delhi.

Krishnaji, N., (1994), "Food Security", Paper presented at the Session 20, International Congress on Kerala Studies, August 27-29, 1994, Thiruvananthapuram, Kerala, Abstracts Vol. 1, pp. 55-56.

Kunhaman, M., (2000),"People's Planning: Planning for a People's Paradigm" Paper presented at the International Conference on Democratic Decentralization, May 2000, State Planning Board, Kerala.

Kurien, C.T., (1994), "Kerala's Development Experience- Some Random Comments about the Past and Some Considerations for the Future".

Loclan, E. and C.Mauffee, (1996), Hegemony and Socialist Strategy: Towards a Radical Democratic Politics, London, Verso.

Logan, K., (1990), 'Women's participation in urban protest'. in Foweraker, J. and Craig, A. (eds). *Popular movements and political change in Mexico.*Boulder: Lynne Rienner, pp. 150-159.

Mahapatra, Bishnu, N., (2001), 'Social Connectedness and Fragility of Social Capital: View from an Orissa Village': *Economic and Political Weekly*, Vol. XXXVI, Feb 24, 2001, p. 665.

Maro, P., (1990), 'The Impact of Decentralisation on Spatial Equity and Rural Development in Tanzania.' *World Development*, 18, pp. 673-693.

Marschak, Thomas, (1959), "Centralisation and Decentralisation in Economic Organisation" *Econometrica*, Vol. 27(3) July.

Martin, J., (1989), 'Mother hood and Power : The Production of women's Politics in a Mexican Community,' *American Ethnologist* 17, pp. 470-490.

Mayer, Murkus, (2001) "Poverty, Local Planning and Youth Empowerment in Southern Sreelanka" Paper presented at the International Conference on Democratic

Decentralisation, May 2000, State Planning Board, Thiruvananthapuram, Kerala.

Mayo, M. and G. Craig, (1995), "Community Participation and Empowerment : The Human face of Structural Adjustment Tools for Democratic transformation in G.Craig and M.Mayo (eds) Community Empowerment: A Reader in Participation and Development. London, Zed.

Mencher, Jean, P., (1994), "The Kerala Model of Development: The Excluded Ones" Paper presented at the Session 7, International Congress on Kerala Studies, August 27-29, 1994, Thiruvananthapuram, Kerala.

Midgley, J., (1986), *Community Participation, Social Development and the State,* Landon: Mathuen.

Mohan, Giles, (1996), "Adjustment and Decentralisation in Ghana, A Case Study of Diminished Soveriegnity", *Political Geography,* 15, 1, pp. 75-94.

Mohan, Giles and Kristian, Stokke, (2000), "Development and Empowerment: The Dangers of Localism" Paper presented at the International Conference on Democratic Decentralisation, May 2000, Trivandrum, Kerala.

Mohanan Pilla, P., (1994), "Small Scale Industries in Kerala : Retrospect and Prospect" International Congress on Kerala Studies, Abstracts Vol. 2, pp. 65-66,August 27-29, 1994, Thiruvananthapuram, Kerala.

Molyneux, M., (1985), "Mobilisation without Emancipation ? Women's Interests, State and Revolution in Nicaragua" *Feminist Studies,* Vol. II, No. 2.

Moser, C., (1987), Mobilisation is Women's Work : Struggles for infrastructure in Guayquil, Ecuador. IN Moser, C and Peake, L.(eds) *Women, Human Settlements and Housing.* London :Tavistock. pp.166-194.

Moser, C., (1989), "*Gender Planning in the Third World: Meeting Practical and Strategic Gender Needs,*' World Development, 17, pp. 1799-1825.

Mosse, D., (1995), "Authority, Gender and Knowledge. Theoretical Reflections on Participatory Rural Appraisal' *Economic and Political Weekly* March 18, pp. 569-578.

Mosse, D., (1997), "The Social Contradictions of People's Knowledge in Participatory Rural Development" in Sunil, Bastian and Nicola, Bastian, (Ed): (1997): *Assessing*

Participation : A debate from South Asia Konark,New Delhi, 1997.

Mridul, Eapen, (1994), "Employment and Unemployment in Kerala: An Analysis of Recent Times" Paper presented at the Session 17, International Congress on Kerala Studies, August 27-29, 1994, Thiruvananthapuram, Kerala.

Mungai Lenneiye, (2000), 'Testing Community Empowring Strategies in Zimbabwe: Examples from Nutrition Supplementation, Water Supply and Sanitation Programmes' *IDS Bulletin*, Vol 31,Number 1, January 2000, Institute of Development Studies, Sussex, pp. 21-30.

Muraleedharan, K., (2000a), "Dynamics of Womens Participation in Development : The Kerala Experience", Paper presented at the International Conference on Democratic Decentralisation, May 2000, State Planning Board, Kerala.

Muraleedharan, K., (2000b), "Womens Participation in Develop-ment : A Study of Dynamics of Women's Participation in the Local Level Planning of Kerala' *Asian Economic Review*, Vol.42, August 2000, No. 2. pp. 338-353.

Muraleedharan, K., (2000c), "Participatory Planning in Kerala: Addressing some basic Questions" Paper presented at 'Decentralised Planning : An Assessment;, the Workshop organised by KRPLLD, CDS, Thiruvananthapuram, Kerala during October 2001.

Muraleedharan, K., (2001), "Women's Participation in Develop-ment and Capacity Builiding at Grass root Level: Some Observations from Kerala" IN S.P.Jain (Eds) *Emerging Institutions for Decentralised Developoment.* Vol. II, NIRD, Hyderabad.

Muraleedharan, K., (2002), "Community Particpation in Decenralised Planning: Some Observations from Empirical Evidences" Paper presented at the 34th Annual Conference of Regional Science Conference held at Dr.John Mathai Center, Aranattukara, Thrissur, Kerala during Dec. 25 to 26 2002.

Musgrave. R.A., (1959), *The theory of Public Finance*, Mac Graw Hill, New York.

Nair, N.D.G., (2000), "People's Planning in Kerala: A Case Study of Two Villages Panchayats". Discussion Paper No. 16. Kerala Research Programme on Local Level Development,

Center for Development Studies, Thiruvananthapuram, Kerala- 695011, Kerala, India.www/http.krpcds.org.

Narayan, J.P., (1961), *Swaraj for the People,* Serve Seva Sangh, Varanasi.

Natraj, Lalitha, (1986), *An Analysis into Political Aspects of Planning in India, New Delhi: Inter India.*

Nicholas, S. Hopkins, (eds.) (1976), *Popular Participation in Social Change.* The Hague: Mouton Publishers.

Niraja Gopal Jayal, (2001), 'Democracy and Social Capital in Central Himalaya: Tale of Two Villages' Economic and Political Weekly, Vol.XXXVI, Feb 24, 2001. pp.655-664.

Nussbaum, Martha, (2003), "Gender and Governance: An Introduction" in Martha Nussbaum (ed) *Essays on Gender and Governance*" HRDC, UNDP India Source: www.undp. org.pub.

Oakely. P.,et. al (1991), *Projects with Peple: The Practice in Rural Development,* ILO, Geneva.

Oakely, R. and Marsdon, D., (1984), *Approaches to Participation in Rural Development,* ILO., Geneva.

Oates, E.W., (1972), *Fiscal Federalism,* Harcount Brace Jouvanovich, New York.

Palanithurai, K.N., (2000), "Democratic Decentralisation in Tamilnadu: A Status Paper".

Parpart, J., (1993), 'Who is the 'other' ? A Post modern Feminist Critique of Women and development Theory and Practice', *Development and Change,* 24, pp. 439-64.

Parpart, J., (2000), "Rethinking Participatory Empowerment, Gender and Development in a Global/Local World" Paper presented at the Conference organized by Center for Developing-Area Studies, McGill University, 20-23 September 2000.

Patil, V.T. and Kittur, A.T., (1990), "Grass Roots Democracy: Analysis of Grama Sabhas" *Political Science Review,* Department of Political Science, University of Rajasthan, Jaipur, Jan-Dec.

Patnaik, (2000), "Alternative Pardigms of Economic Decentrlisatioin "Paper presented at the International Conference on Democratic Decentralisation, May 2000, State Planning Board, Kerala.

Patrick Heller, (2000), "*Moving the State: The Politics of Decentralisation in Kerala,South Africa and Porto Alegre*". Paper presented at the International Conference on Democratic Decentralisation, May 2000, State Planning Board, Kerala.

Paul, E., (1993), "Prospectus for Liberalisation in Singapore", *Journal of Contemprory Asia*, 23, pp. 1871-5.

Paul, S., (1986), *Community Participation in Development Projects-the World Bank Experiences* : WB, Discussion Paper 6.

Paulo, Freire, (1996), Pedagogy of the Oppressed, Penguin, Landon.

Pearse, Andrews and Stiefel, Mathias, (1979), "Inquiry in to Participation : A Research Approach" *Popular Participation Programme*, The United Nations Research Institute for Social Development, (UNRISD): 1979, p. 5.

Pijnenburg, B. and Nhantumbo, I., (2002), *Participatory development interventions in Mozambique*. Development in Practice. 2002 May;12(2), pp.192-9.

Pretty, J., et. al (1994), "Alternative Systems for Inquiry for a Sustainable Agriculture" IDS Bulletine, 25 (2).

Putnam, Robert, (1993), *Making Democracy Work: Civic Traditions in Modern italy*, Princeton, University Press.

Radcliff, S. and Westwood, S., (eds) (1996), *Women and Popular protests in Latin America* New York: Routledge.

Raghavan, P., (1994), "Traditional Industries in Kerala: the Need for New Approaches" International Congress on Kerala Studies, Abstracts Vol. 2, pp. 30-31, August 27-29, 1994, Thiruvananthapuram, Kerala.

Raj, K.N., (1992), "Decentralised Development and local Self Government in Kerala" Paper presented at the seminar on Panchayat Raj/Nagar Palika Bill and its Implications for Local Self Governments and Decentralized Development in Kerala" October 2-3, Center for Development Studies, Thiruvananthapuram, Kerala, India.

Raj, K.N., (1971), "Planning from below with Reference to District Development and State Planning". *Economic and Political Weekly*, VI, Nos. 30-32.

Rajan Gurukkal, (2000), "Coalition of Conflicting Interests and the Politics of Decentralisation: A therectic Critique". Paper presented at the International Conference on Democratic Decentralisation, May 2000, State Planning Board, Kerala.

Ralf, Strakloff, (1997), "Participatory Discourses and Practice in a Water Resource Crisis in Sri Lanka' in Sunil, Bastian and Nicola, Bastian, (Ed) (1997): *Assessing Participation: A debate from South Asia* New Delhi, 1997.

Ramachandran, (1994), "Kerala in Institute of Social Sciences: 1994, Status of Panchayat Raj in the States of India 1994" Concept, New Delhi.

Raphel, Jos, C., (1990), "Decentralized Planning in Karnataka" (Mimeo), Centre for Development Studies and Activities, Pune.

Renata, Serra, (2001), "Social Capital : Meaningful and Measurable at the State Level', *Economic and Political Weekly*, Vol. XXXVI, Feb 24, 2001. pp. 693-695.

Rene Loewenson, (2000) "Public Participation in Health" *IDS Bulletin*, Volume 31, No. 1, January 2000.

Rex, A. Cassainder, (1994), "Enigma of Kerala Spatial Formations : Gragara and an Invalidation/Recovery of Desakota Hypothesis" Paper presented at the Session 20, International Congress on Kerala Studies, August 27-29, 1994, Thiruvananthapuram, Kerala,

Rondinelli, D., McCullough, J., and R. Johnson, (1989), "Analysing Decentralisation Policies in Developing Countries: A Political-Economy framework" *Development and Change*, 20, pp. 57-87.

Sachidanandam, Shanti, (1997), "Participatory Appraisal of Development under Civil War Conditions: The Experience of Batticaloa, Sree Lanka,1991- 1995" in Sunil, Bastian and Nicola, Bastian, (Ed) (1997): *Assessing Participation: A debate from South Asia* New Delhi, 1997.

Samoff, J., (1990), "Decentralisation: the politics of Interventionism'. *Development and Change*, 21, pp. 513-530.

Samaranayake, Mallika, (1997), 'Significance of Participatory Approaches in Empowering People for Sustainable Development' in Sunil Bastian and Nicola, Bastian, (Ed)

(1997): *Assessing Participation: A debate from SouthAsia* Konark, New Delhi, 1997.

Sen, Amartya, (1999), *Development as Freedom*, Alfred. A. Knopt, New York.

Sharma, Rashmi, (2003), "Kerala's Decentralization; Idea in Practice" *Economic and Political Weekly, Sept. 6, 2003*, pp. 3832-50.

Simon, D. and Rakodi, C., (1990), Conclusions and Prospects: What future for regional planning ? in Simon, D (ed):, *Third Word Regional Development: A Reappraisal*. London; Chapman, pp. 249-260.

Singh, J.P. Vyas, N.N. Mann, R.S., (ed).(1988), *Tribal Women and Development* Rawat; Jaipur.

Singh, Yatindra, (2002), "Decentralised Governance in M.P. Experience of the Gram Sabha in Scheduled Areas" *Economic and Political Weekly*, Oct. 5, pp. 4100-4104.

Slater, D.C., (1989), "Territorial Power and the Peripheral States: The Issue of Decentralisation" *Devleopment and Change*, 20, pp. 501-531.

Smith, M.G., (1975), *Corporations and Society*, Chicago: Aldina publishing Company: pp. 133-163.

Smith, B., (1985), *Decentralisation: The Territorial Dimensons of State*. London: Allen and Unwin.

Sreekumar, T.T., (1994), "Understanding Spatial Divide in Kerala" Paper presented at the Session 20, International Congress on Kerala Studies, August 27-29, 1994, Thiruvananthapuram, Kerala.

State Planning Board (1997) "The People's Campaign for Ninth Plan in Kerala: An Introduction" Government of Kerala., Thiruvananthapuram.

Stephen, L., (1989), *Not Just One of the Boys : from Female to Feminist in Popular Rural Movements in Mexico*. Paper Delivered at the Annual Meeting s of LASA (Latin American Studies Association): Pureto Rico.

Stirrat, R.L., (1997), "The New Orthodoxy and Truths: Particiipation, Empowerment and other Buzz Words" in Sunil, Bastian and Nicola, Bastian, (Ed) (1997): *Assessing Participation: A debate from South Asia*, New Delhi.

Stohr, W., (1981), *Development from Below: The bottom-up and Periphery-Inward Development Paradigm.* Chichester; Wiley.

Stohr and Tailor, D., (eds) (1981), *Development from Above or Below ? The Dialectics of Regional Planning in Developing Countries* Chichester: Wiley.

Stokke, Kristian (1998), "Globalisation and the Politics of Poverty Alleviation in the South". Norvegean Journal of Geography, 52, pp. 221-228.

Subramanian K.K. and Mohanan Pillai, P., (1986), "Kerala's Industrial Backwardness: Exploration of Alternative Hypothesis" *Economic and Political Weekly,* Vol. 21, No.14, April 5, pp. 577-92.

Subramanian, K.K., (1994), "Industrial Strategy for Kerala: A Perspective" International Congress on Kerala Studies, August 27-29, 1994, Thiruvananthapuram, Kerala, Abstracts-A, Vol. II, pp. 19-20.

Sudha, Pai, (2001), "Social Capital, Panchayaths and Grass Roots Demcocracy: Politics of Dalit Assertion in Uttarpradesh'. Economic and Political Weekly, Vol. XXXVI, Feb 24, 2001, pp. 646-654.

Sutton, P., (1989), *Development Ideology, its Emergence and Decline*, Deadulus, 118, 3pp.5-67.

Tharakan, Michael.P.K., (1994), "Search for Roots of Kerala 'Model' in Colonial and Pre-Colonial History',, Paper presented at the Session 42, , International Congress on Kerala Studies, August 27-29, 1994, Thiruvananthapuram, Kerala.

Tharakan, Michael, P.K., (1992), "Socio–Religious Reform Movements and Demand for Indicators of Development: Thiruvithamkoor, 1860-1930. in Alok Bhalla and Peer Bumke, *Image of Rural India in the 20th Century.* Sterling Publishers, New Delhi.

Tharamangalam, Joseph, (1998), "The Perils of Social Development without Economic Growth; the Development Debacle of Kerala, India. *Bulletin of Concerned Asian Scholars.* Vol. 30, No. 1,July- September, pp. 23-33.

Tornquist, Olle, (1999), *Politics and Development: A Critical Introduction,* Sage Publications, London. pp. 145-6.

Turner, Mark and Hulme, David, (1997), Governance, Administration and Development. Making the Sate Work. 1997, Kumerian Press, West Hartford, p. 159.

Umadevi, S., (1994), "Critical Comments on Kerala Model of Development" Paper presented at the Session 7, International Congress on Kerala Studies, August 27-29, 1994, Thiruvananthapuram, Kerala.

United Nations, (1981), "Popular Participation as a Strategy for Promoting Country Level Action and Natural Development, New York, UNP.

United Nations, (UN) and Center for Development Studies (CDS) (1975), *Poverty Unemployment and Development Policy: A Case Study of Selected Issues with Reference to Kerala.* Department of Economic and Social Affairs, UN, New York.

Uphoff, Norman, T. and Cohen, John, (1977), *Rural Development Participipation: Concepts and Measures for Project Design Implementation and Evaluation,* Ithaca: Cornell University, 1977.

Uphoff, Norman.T. and Esmann, Milton, J., (1986), "Local Organisation for Rural Development : Analysis of Asian Experiences" .Ithaca: Cornell University, Center for International Studies, Rural Development Committee, Special Series on Rural Local Government, No. 19.

Vengroff, R., and Johnston, A., (1989), 'Decentralisation and the Implementation of Rural Development 'in Senegal : *The View from Below.* New York: Edwin Mellen.

Vettivel, S.K., (1999), *Particpation: Concept, Approaches and Techniques, New Delhi, Vetri,* New Delhi.

Wignaraja, P., (1991), "Genesis of Intellectual Quest: An Overview", Wignaraja, P., Hussain. A, Sethi. H., Wignaraja, G. (co authors) *Participatory Development: Learning from South Asia.,* Oxford University Press.

William Tordoff, (1994), "Decentralisation, Comparative Experience in Common Wealth Africa, Journal of Modern African Studies, Vol. 32, No. 4, pp. 555-580.

Wolf, Eric, R., (1977), "Kinship, Friendship and Patron-Client Relations in Complex Societies" In Staffen.W.Schmidt, Laura Guasti, Carol.H.Lande and James.C.Scott. (Eds),

Friends,Followers and Factions. Berkely: University of California Press, 1977.

World Bank (1990), "Strengthening Local Governments in Sub Saharan Africa "EDI Policy Seminar. Report Series 21, Washington D.C, WB.

World Bank (1997), *World Development Report : The State in a Changing World,* Oxford, Oxford University Press.

Wright (2000), "Envisioning Real Uttopias" Paper presented at the International Conference on Democratic Decentralisa-tion. State Planning Board, Thiruvananthapuram, Kerala, India.

Zacharia, K.C., (1994), "Demographic Transition in Kerala: A Response to Official Policies and Programmes" Paper presented at the Session 19. International Congress on Kerala Studies, August 27-29, 1994, Thiruvananthapuram, Kerala.

Zesuliwe Mkhize (2000), "Decentralisation: A Grassroots Perspective". Paper presented at the International Conference on Democratic Decentralisation, May 2000, State Planning Board, Kerala.